W9-BFP-633

STEAMSHIPS and MOTORSHIPS

of the

WEST COAST

MATSON LINE PASSENGER FLEET passing under the Golden Gate Bridge (Superimposed.)
Top to bottom: STEAMSHIPS the former *Lurline*, *Monterey*, new *Lurline*, and *Mariposa*.

—*Matson Navigation Company*

STEAMSHIPS
and MOTORSHIPS
of the West Coast

A Story in Pictures and Words
About
Some Famous and Unusual Vessels
Along the Pacific Coast
of
North America

BY RICHARD M. BENSON

Bonanza Books • New York

FIRST SAVANNAH

—Malcolm Bell, Jr.
for the Pigeonhole Press

Copyright © MCMLXVIII by Superior Publishing Co.
Library of Congress Catalog Card Number: 68-22360
All rights reserved.
This edition is published by Bonanza Books
a division of Crown Publishers, Inc.
by arrangement with Superior Publishing Company
a b c d e f g h

DEDICATION

To my wife, Edla.

FOREWORD

THIS BOOK DEALS with certain merchant steamships or motorships, either American or foreign, most of which have appeared at one time or another at ports along our Pacific Coast. Different types of vessels are described in non-technical terms, the aim being to enlist the love of ships as a first step in following the sea.

A brief history of steamship development on the Pacific Coast is offered in the way of background for the story of present-day steamship and motorship operation. This unfoldment also includes the subject of ferries that always arouses an interest in people. A few marine disasters are described in Chapter IV to indicate that the ever-present dangers of the sea are always with us.

Much of the material in the book's chapter dealing with pioneer vessels, early-day ferries, and ship disasters has been told more fully elsewhere in printed form.

Another feature of the book is that it rather briefly indicates the different types of cargo carrying vessels that visited our ports up to the year 1967. The final chapter "Ships of Tomorrow" attempts to outline the transition from the old type of vessel to the new in terms of outward appearance, motive power, and other changes.

Many steamship companies by 1968 were beginning to bring out vessels of newer design and larger in size. The next decade or so will see changes in design that are unknown today.

In all, the book hopes to briefly portray the past and present, in line with steamship and motorship development along the Pacific Coast of North America.

CONTENTS

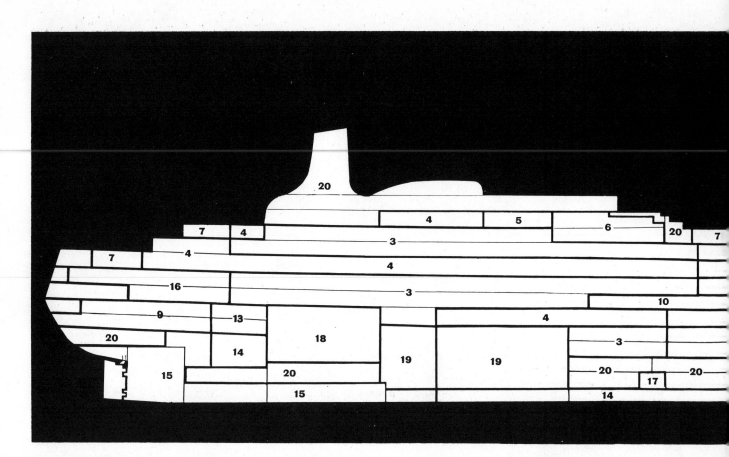

Acknowledgments

The AUTHOR is greatly indebted to the steamship men up and down the coast for their wonderful cooperation in supplying me with pictures and factual material dealing with either their vessels or company operations.

The Lewis and Dryden and the H. W. McCurdy Marine Histories of the Pacific Northwest have been extremely important reference material.

He also thanks James Gibbs, editor of the fine marine publication, the *Marine Digest,* for permission to use many interesting accounts of shipping on this coast.

Thanks are also extended to various marine photographers and to staff members of historical societies who went out of their way to supply me with pictures that I did not think were available. This was particularly true with the pictures supplied me from the historical collection of the Union Title Insurance and Trust Company of San Diego.

The author appreciates the granting of permission to use material from a previous article of mine published in the *Peninsula Living*.

ILLUSTRATION OF INTERIOR of the passenger vessel, *SS Canberra*.

 1. 1st Class Staterooms
 2. 1st Class Public Rooms
 3. Tourist Staterooms
 4. Tourist Public Rooms
 5. Nurseries
 6. Cinema
 7. Swimming Pools
 8. Galley
 9. Laundry
10. Hospital
11. Bridge
12. Cargo and Baggage Handling Equipment
13. Cargo Holds, Baggage and Storerooms
14. Fuel and Ballast Tanks
15. Fresh Water
16. Crew Accommodation
17. Stabilizers
18. Boilers
19. Main Engines
20. Auxiliary Engines

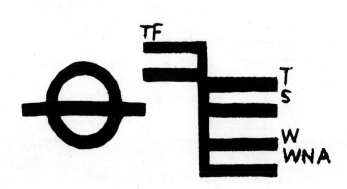

PLIMSOLL MARK

Chapter I

There's Something About a Ship...

INTEREST IN SHIPS of one type or another has existed as long as there has been transportation by water. Some of the early-day vessels were both crude in design and slow in performance. Later on, others became a thing of beauty and were often noted for their speed. Today's stress on cargo carrying capacity has tended to limit graceful lines and general beauty.

Steamships thus can be easily dated by their general appearance. The newer cargo liners and passenger vessels of recent times show streamlining effects to conform to the modern idea of design. The older vessels tend to have wider beams and stand higher in the water. Cargo vessels of today often carry one fat funnel, instead of the tall, black funnel of yesteryear. The steamships of still earlier days had two to four funnels in order to provide enough natural draft for the engine room. As the years have gone by the extra funnels and sail masts have about disappeared. On some motorships, false funnels have been fitted to give proper balance to the ship's profile. Early-day Diesel driven motorships displayed no funnels whatsoever. Quite a stir was created by one of the first motorships, back in 1912, when the Danish ship *Selandia* appeared with three masts but no funnels. This was done purposely so that she would be recognized as a motorship. In the chapter on "Ships of Tomorrow", you will note the odd funnel arrangement of two of the P & O-Orient Lines vessels, the *SS Oriana* and the *SS Canberra*. The *Canberra* has two slim funnels arranged side by side at the stern of the ship much like some of the modern-day tankers. Engine rooms show vast change in the matter of ship's propulsion. The first steamboats used steam as the only source of power, which in turn drove a paddle wheel located either at the stern or on the side of the vessel. The next period of transition was from the paddle wheel to the screw propeller. The single propeller has been widely used through the years. Twin, or even triple propellers, have been fitted to larger passenger liners to provide greater speed of operation.

The first sea-going vessel to be propelled by a Diesel engine was the motorship *Vulcanus* back in 1910. She was a tanker built by the Dutch and operated by them in the Netherlands-East Indies trade. The *Vulcanus* was propelled by a 6-cylinder single acting engine. She served until 1931 when she was broken up. But her engine was still in perfect condition.

At the present time a nautical mile represents 6,076.10333 feet as compared to an even 5,280 feet in statute miles. This became official for the United States in 1954, making a nautical mile approximately 796 feet longer than a statute mile. It does not make much of a difference in terms of one mile, but it does make quite a difference in the distance covered by a ship in a period of twenty-four hours.

A LARGE DIESEL ENGINE. An example of the immense size of a Diesel engine for a large cargo or passenger vessel.

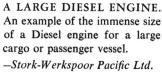
—Stork-Werkspoor Pacific Ltd.

The fastest American passenger liner, the *United States,* presently holds a record with the registered average speed of 35.59 knots, or nautical miles per hour, in crossing the Atlantic. Many warships can travel 40 knots or more. Some modern cargo ships of today can travel between 18 and 25 knots. Many passenger liners are designed to cruise at 27 knots.

A vessel is fully loaded when she is "down to her marks" which means all the weight she can safely carry. How much a vessel can carry, or be lawfully

submerged, is determined by her *load line*. This line is determined by the ship's builders, "officially measured and then engraved on the ship's plates and painted white."[1]

"Coincident with the load line on the side of a vessel is the *Plimsoll Mark*. This mark takes its name from a member of the British Parliament who caused it to be officially adopted in Britain as a measure of a vessel's safe loading in any water and in any season."[2]

"To the left of the vertical line of the Plimsoll

mark are depths to which the vessel may be loaded in fresh water, "F", and Tropical fresh water, "TF". A vessel loaded in fresh water to the mark "F" will immediately lessen its draft to mark "S" as it enters the ocean and is buoyed up by denser salt water. On the salt water side of the line, the vessel may be loaded according to season to "T" in the tropics, to "S" in summertime, to "W" in wintertime and only to "WNA" when her voyage will be in the North Atlantic in wintertime. The marks apply when the voyage is in the ocean, but a vessel loading in fresh water to proceed to sea is given allowance to compensate for the difference in densities of the waters to be encountered.

"The distances between the lines in the Plimsoll mark vary slightly with each vessel. For a liberty-type ship the distance between "S" and "W" is seven inches. This means that a fully loaded Liberty ship can lawfully load in summer 343 more long tons of cargo than she can in winter."[3]

Considerable change has taken place with respect to the interior of a ship in the way of crew's quarters and passenger accommodations. The early-day side wheelers in the ocean trade had their cabin space mostly below decks. Later early-day steamers had cabins fitted to accommodate about sixty first-class passengers. The staterooms, though small, were well furnished for their day. Some of these cabins opened into the first-class lounge and some to the deck. The steerage passengers were accommodated in very plain quarters between decks where they had a common mess hall for dining.

The early-day ship's galley served two meals a day to both cabin class and steerage. In the steerage mess hall they were divided into groups of about twenty people, each group having a mess captain. This individual was responsible for securing the food for his mess group, which generally consisted of hot liquids in one large container and hot cooked solid foods in another and dispensed these to his group.

Today, the luxury liners have several decks extending upward from the main deck. The passenger cabins are often arranged in tiers according to first or second-class accommodations. Wide glass enclosed verandas, or decks, are built around the superstructure affording protection from the winds while the vessel is at sea. In the old days there were three classes, first, second, and steerage. The latter class, which was mainly reserved for immigrants, has about disappeared from the high seas. Today one finds some vessels that are strictly one class and these ships are employed in the regular season travel and then rerouted for the winter cruise trade. Passenger travel along the Pacific Coast has just about disappeared for

CLOSE-UP OF A SHIP'S PROPELLER. The size of the propeller can be seen by the man standing by.

—Burrard Dry Dock Co., Ltd.

A GALLEY RANGE. An example of a heavy duty oil burning galley range. Note the three oven doors and the guard rails on top to hold pots and pans during rough weather at sea.

—The Montague Company

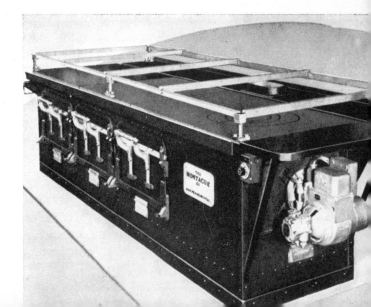

SS METAPAN. A banana boat being assisted into her berth.
—*Mike McGarvey*

American vessels. The early part of this century saw a live passenger trade between ports from San Diego up the coast to Puget Sound, and even to Alaska. Those were the days of the Pacific Coast Steamship liners, and later the "Alexander" fleet of which were the famous steamships *H. F., Ruth, Emma,* and *Dorothy Alexander.* Those were also the days of the famous *Harvard* and *Yale,* whose white passenger ships sailed out of San Francisco to Los Angeles and San Diego.

Most vessels built today are of steel or aluminum and thus have a cool, hard feeling in their appearance. A naval architect, a woman, is trying and most successfully to restore the sea-like appearance and feeling of the interior of new ships that are being built.

Not long ago, she designed the interiors of three mariner-type cargo vessels for the American President Lines. These included the *Presidents Polk, Monroe,* and *Harrison.* In designing the quarters for the passengers and crew, she used wood exclusively in her plans. This was to give the feeling of a ship. Even walnut floors were put in some of the staterooms and wooden panels in the dining room. The wood was coated with a thin layer of vinyl making it fireproof. She also gives her vessels the old sea-faring look by installing brass and mahogany binnacles, antique eagles, fish pond tables, old seamen's chests, and 18th century prints giving an authentic touch to the public rooms.

The modern steamship or motorship, whether it be passenger or freighter, is often air-conditioned, has spacious rooms in the form of staterooms, and even in the crew's quarters where two crewmen to a room with a shower is not unusual. This is quite a contrast to the old days when the crewmen were housed in stuffy quarters in either the forecastle, or below decks in other parts of the ship.

Public rooms of modern day ships are both functional and serve as an area of recreation while at sea. One of these is the dining room where excellent food

MV SAGA MARU. A Japanese cargo liner sails under the Golden Gate Bridge.
—*Nippon Yusen Kaisha Line*

OSWEGO VICTORY. A tanker heads into a moderate sea.
—*Arabian American Oil Company*

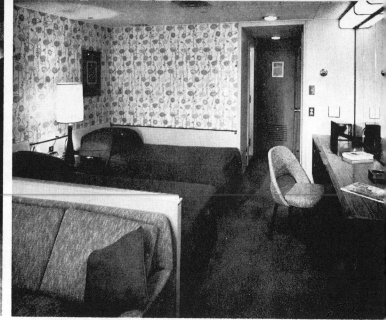

DINING ROOM SCENE. *SS President Cleveland.*
—*American President Line*

STATEROOM SCENE. *SS President Roosevelt.* In the de luxe staterooms of today, beds are now used instead of bunks one above the other.
—*American President Line*

is to be had. The preparation of food in the ship's galley has undergone tremendous change since the early days. At one time, the stove consisted of an open platform lined with stone. A tripod supported the kettle which hung over a charcoal brazier. Today most vessel's galleys represent a typical restaurant on land with oil fired or electric stoves.

On the deck of a modern steamship, or motorship, hatches are noticed fore and aft for the storage of cargo, either dry or in liquid form. Cranes, originally operated by hand, then steam, and finally by electricity, serve as an important part of the vessel. Ships carrying grain, or similar cargo, use suction pipes for its removal from the ship and its pipe system is reversed while loading. Moving belts, or elevators, are used to unload fruit such as bananas. Liquids carried in the form of gasoline, oil, and chemicals are conveyed by pipes under a pressure system from the wharf or vessel. Since much cargo is carried in huge vans, or containers, especially large cranes are needed on board the vessel or on the wharf.

Another interesting piece of equipment found on the deck of many ships is a machine that keeps the mooring lines in constant tension. This allows the vessel to remain securely moored during the change of tides.

It may be of interest to note at this point how a ship is accepted after it has been built. What regulations help the owner to know his ship is ready for use? The *"Marine Digest"* lists the following rules for the acceptance of sea trials:

1. Efficiency of the steam or Diesel plant
2. Measurement of horsepower
3. Economy and endurance runs
4. Anchoring
5. Circling and steering

The agencies approving the above trials are the ship builder, the Maritime Administration, the American Bureau of Shipping, and the Coast Guard.

There are several navigational aids that are of value in operating a ship. First, it has always been customary to take the ship's position daily at noon. This is done by taking the meridian altitude sight of the sun at its zenith. From this the latitude and longitude of the vessel's position is computed. During cloudy, or bad weather, the ship's position is determined by dead reckoning by use of sea charts.

Modern ships carry two types of compasses. One is a gyro compass, which is a very exact machine activated by a gyroscope and which keeps the compass needle constantly pointed at true north.

The other compass is called a magnetic compass whose needle is activated by the earth's magnetism. In this case the needle points to the magnetic pole which lies south of the geographic north pole. The purpose is to provide a check of one compass against the other.

Another recent navigational aid is the radar screen which reposes in the pilothouse where officers can observe an oncoming vessel and watch its progress. The antenna for the radar is usually located on a high point above the pilothouse.

SS JAPAN MAIL. *SS Japan Mail plows into a heavy sea.*
—*American Mail Line*

A SHIP'S COMPASS. Two passengers are learning the purpose of the compass from a ship's officer.

—*American President Line*

SS PHILIPPINE MAIL. American Mail Line vessel in Seattle's Elliott Bay.

—American Mail Line

A		ALFA I am undergoing a speed trial.	**N**		NOVEMBER No (negative).
B		BRAVO I am taking in or dis- charging explosives.	**O**		*OSCAR Man overboard.
C		CHARLIE Yes (affirmative)	**P**		*PAPA IN HARBOUR—All persons to repair on board; vessel about to proceed to sea. AT SEA—Your lights are out or burn- ing badly.
D		DELTA Keep clear of me—I am manoeuvring with difficulty.	**Q**		QUEBEC My vessel is healthy, and I require free pratique.
E		ECHO I am directing my course to starboard.	**R**		*ROMEO The way is off my ship—you may feel your way past me.
F		*FOXTROT I am disabled—com- municate with me.	**S**		SIERRA My engines are going full speed astern.
G		GOLF I require a pilot.	**T**		TANGO Do not pass ahead of me.
H		HOTEL I have a pilot on board.	**U**		*UNIFORM You are standing into danger.
I		INDIA I am directing my course to port.	**V**		*VICTOR I require assistance.
J		JULIET I am going to send a message by semaphore.	**W**		*WHISKEY I require medical assistance.
K		*KILO You should stop your vessel instantly.	**X**		X-RAY Stop carrying out intentions and watch for my signals.
L		*LIMA You should stop—I have some- thing important to communicate.	**Y**		YANKEE I am carrying mails.
M		MIKE I have a doctor on board.	**Z**		*ZULU To be used to address or call shore stations.

Only those letters and meanings marked * may be indicated by the Morse Code either by sound or by flashing.

SIGNAL FLAGS. The flags are actually in color. The Morse Code and the message for each flag is found on the chart on the right-hand page.

—*Vancouver Tug Boat Co., Ltd.*

COVERED BARGES
Queens of the VT fleet, which have revolutionized paper products transportation.

LUMBER SCOWS
and other stanchion-sided scows for miscellaneous hauling.

BULK CARRIERS
With capacities up to 3200 tons.

CHIP SCOWS
Our flotilla of log and chip scows—including 15 new 700-unit vessels with more under construction—is the largest in the Pacific Northwest.

YELLOW
RED
BLUE

An informative guide to International Code Signals is yours for the asking. Just drop us a note to Dept. IC, Vancouver Tug Boat Co. Ltd., 555 Denman Street, Vancouver.

VICTORIA EV2-2155   COURTENAY 331
NANAIMO SK3-4511   WESTVIEW HU2-3451

VANCOUVER
TUG BOAT Co· L™
VANCOUVER, BRITISH COLUMBIA

VANCOUVER BARGE
TRANSPORTATION LTD.

OFFICER "SHOOTING THE SUN." The ship's position is taken at noon by a sextant which gives the operator a chance to measure the angular distance from the sun and thus determine his vessel's latitude at sea.

—*American President Line*

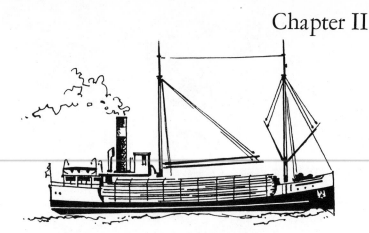

Chapter II

Some Pioneer Vessels on the Pacific Coast

DURING THE COURSE OF 125 years of steamship development along the Pacific Coast, many a steamship pioneered some type of trade or service. Some vessels were either the first to enter a new trade route, or were one of the first of its type to offer a new kind of service.

Shortly after the first crossing of the Atlantic by the American steamship *Savannah,* in 1819, little steamboats began to venture into the Pacific Ocean. There were three of these historic vessels; namely, the *Telica,* the *Sophia Jane,* and the *Beaver.* The honor of being the first ship in the Pacific goes to the *Telica.* She arrived in 1825 at the sleepy little port of Guayaquil, in Ecuador, South America, where she was fitted with a steam engine carried in her hold. From this port, the *Telica* proceeded northward up the coast only to run into a dense fog and also ran out of fuel for her boiler. This was too much for her passengers. As the story has it, a Spaniard by the name of Mitzovich, became so disgusted with the turn of events that he fired a pistol into a barrel of gunpowder. The explosion blew the vessel to pieces, killing himself and all aboard except for one man. This was really a sad beginning for steamship travel along the Pacific Coast.

About six years later, a little 251-ton paddle wheeler by the name of *Sophia Jane* surprised everyone one morning in Sydney, Australia, by arriving unannounced on a voyage under steam from far away England.

The third vessel, the *Beaver,* arrived at the mouth of the Columbia River in Oregon and sailed some 100 miles up the river to Fort Vancouver in the year 1836. The *Beaver,* like the *Telica,* came around the Horn with engines in her hold. When the engines had been properly placed in the vessel, the *Beaver* was to become the first steamboat to operate on the coast of North America. She sailed for many years in the fur trade for the famous Hudson's Bay Company. Later the *Beaver* was transferred from the Columbia River northward to British Columbia where she spent her last days. As often happens with an older vessel, the *Beaver* was finally converted into a tugboat. After some fifty years of pioneering service in the Northwest, the *Beaver* ran aground near the entrance to Vancouver and was a total loss.

Being such an historic little vessel, much of her remains were salvaged and saved for souvenirs and other mementos. The Washington Historical Society, at Tacoma, has the *Beaver's* boiler on display. A portion of the poop deck reposes in a museum in Victoria, B. C. The Oregon Historical Society, in Portland, proudly displays fire brick from the engine room of the *Beaver.* And the ship's anchor is housed in the museum at Fort Vancouver.

SS BEAVER. The first steamship to arrive in the Pacific Northwest in 1836.
—*J. A. Casoly*

The Hudson's Bay Company in 1852 ordered the construction in England of a companion ship for the *Beaver*. This vessel was named the *Otter*, which like the *Beaver*, rendered many years of service in British Columbia waters. The *Otter* was a screw vessel of 222 tons, 122 feet long, and drew two feet of water. She arrived in Victoria in 1853 and was placed on the Victoria to New Westminster run. In 1858 the *Otter* and another vessel by the name of the *Sea Bird* made regular trips up the Fraser River from New Westminster. During the Indian War on Puget Sound, the *Otter* was chartered by the United States government to serve as a warship at a stipend of $300 per day. The local Indian tribe was quite taken back at seeing the *Otter* and was quite concerned over the fact that she was not propelled by side wheels like the *Beaver*. The *Otter* sank near Bella Coola at the Northern end of Vancouver Island. She was raised, refitted, and ran for several years until she was dismantled in 1890.

1. COASTWISE TRAVEL

It was not until 1848 that a steamship line, the Pacific Mail of New York, was established to carry mail and passengers from the west side of Panama for settlers living in Oregon and California. For this service, three side-wheelers were built and were named the *California, Oregon,* and *Panama*. By the time the *California* had sailed around the Horn and reached Panama, news had broken out about the discovery of gold in California. In the meantime the prospectors had taken a ship from New York to the east coast of Panama, crossed the jungle on the Isthmus to the port where the *California* was to drop anchor. The *California* was designed to carry about 180 passengers, but when she left Panama she had twice that number! The *California* arrived in San Francisco Bay in February of 1849 making her the first steamship to enter the coastal trade. When the *Oregon* and *Panama* arrived later, they, too, were crowded with prospectors, many of them paying as much as $1,000 for the voyage.

The *SS California* was a typical steamship of her day. Though small by modern standards, she was large and spacious for her day. The *California* was 200 feet long, had a beam of 35 feet, and when registered, tonnage was 1,050. On each side were paddle wheels covered with a housing that extended out beyond the outboard. Her hull was constructed of live

LOT WHITCOMB. One of the first steamboats built in Oregon. She later operated as the *Annie Abernathy* on the Sacramento River in California.
— *Oregon Historical Society*

oak, white oak, and cedar with the bottom sheathed in copper. The vessel was rigged with three masts as a barkentine. Although the *California's* average speed from New York to California was 11.87 knots, the most of the voyage was a relatively slow 8.68 knots. Stormy weather hampered the turning of the paddle wheels, as one paddle wheel would be at times six feet out of the water on one side and buried in the rough sea on the other, all of which caused a strain on both her engines and her hull.

As the gold rush in California progressed, several steamship lines entered the scene to compete with the Pacific Mail, and a brisk business developed between Central American ports and San Francisco. Many of these competing lines disappeared as soon as the gold rush waned and the Pacific Mail again became the lone operator from Panama for many years.

Along the various harbors and rivers on the coast of North America, there were a number of steam vessels of all sizes that pioneered travel in these waters. One of the first steamboats to appear in San Francisco Bay was the Russian-built *Sitka*. This little

vessel had been brought from Alaska to the Russian trading post at Fort Ross above San Francisco. The *Sitka* was short-lived for she sank four months later in San Francisco Bay. She was raised out of the water and spent her last days as a schooner under the name of *Rainbow*.

One Christmas day in 1850 there was launched in Milwaukie on the Willamette, above Portland, a more pretentious steamer called the *Lot Whitcomb*, named for its owner and builder. The *Lot Whitcomb* was a side-wheeler 160 feet long, 24 feet beam, and had a depth of 5 feet 8 inches. Her engine of 140 horsepower gave her a speed of 12 miles per hour. The *Lot Whitcomb* was an expensive boat to operate and was sold in 1854 to the California Steam Navigation Company, where she was placed on the Sacramento River trade as the *Annie Abernathy*.

In the years that were to follow, a lively trade developed on the lower and upper Columbia and its tributary the Willamette. Many of the riverboats carried passengers and general freight. Others were used for towing of various kinds. The first steamer built for towing was the *Oklahoma* and for her day, start-

24

STEAMER POLITKOFSKY. Early-day Russian vessel built in Alaska. This vessel later came under the American flag.
                                                                                    —Seattle Historical Society

ing in the 1875's, she had the longest record for towing of any sternwheeler on the Columbia, until she was taken out of service in 1894.

Those living in this part of Oregon will readily recall the steamers *Claire* and *Henderson*. The *Henderson* had the run for many years from Portland to The Dalles. In 1963, plans were made to demolish this old timer and it is said her boilers, still in good condition, were sold to a South American firm. The *Str. Claire,* built in 1918, ended her career in 1961 when she was buried on a Columbia River sand bar. The *Claire*, "Always a favorite of veteran steamboat men at their reunions," was the last sternwheeler to transit the Willamette Falls locks. She was operated by the Western Transportation Company of Portland.

Smaller towboats have now pretty much replaced the old river steamers with regard to towing and barging. Modern highways and railroads now along both river systems carry the bulk of the freight in these times.

Steamboat development on Puget Sound in Northern Washington likewise was the scene of a lively traffic. This long arm of the sea extending over 100 miles inland proved to be an ideal area for travel by boat. It was here that the famous "mosquito fleet" was created to serve various ports around the Sound. The term "mosquito," in this case, refers to literally hundreds of small boats that operated between such places as Port Townsend, Bellingham, Seattle, Tacoma, Olympia and others. Like the river boats they carried passengers and freight.

One of the first steamboats to appear on Puget Sound was a little side-wheeler called the *Fairy*. This little vessel, which arrived on the Sound in 1853, was actually unloaded from a sailing vessel that had sailed up the coast from San Francisco as she was too small to make such an ocean voyage.

The *Fairy* used Olympia as her home port and attempted to operate between that town and Seattle. It was on this run that the little vessel got into difficulties. On her regular run, as she rounded Alki Point at the entrance to Seattle's harbor, she would lay over on her side with one paddle wheel turning out of the water. This caused no end of concern among the passengers who figured that the fare between the two ports didn't warrant being frightened to death.

Early-day transportation by water in British Columbia, following the arrival of the *Beaver* and the *Otter,* for many years was a slow one. The towns of Victoria and New Westminster preceded that of Vancouver, which city did not come into its own until the arrival of the Canadian Pacific Railroad in 1887. At the turn of the century fast modern passenger liners were built for what then became the famous triangular route; namely, between Vancouver to Victoria to Seattle and return. For this service the Canadian Pacific Railroad placed a whole array of "Princess" steamships for this run. Some of these vessels included the *Princesses Alice, Louise, Victoria, Elizabeth, Charlotte,* and the surviving *Marguerite* and *Patricia.* The latter steamship in recent years has been used exclusively in the Alaskan trade and as a cruise ship to Mexico in 1965-1966. The *Marguerite* no longer is on the triangular run, but presently operates between Seattle and Victoria.

On the traveled routes in recent years was a competitor of the Canadian Pacific Railroad in the form of a line of "Prince" steamships operated by the Canadian Grand Trunk Railway and now operating as the Canadian National Steamship Company. Perhaps the most famous of this line was the *Prince Rupert,* which with her three funnels was a familiar sight in British Columbia waters and Seattle. Other vessels in this fleet were the *Prince David,* and *Prince George,* which were also three-stackers.

Another important steamship company that had a large part in developing steamship trade in British Columbia waters was the Union Steamship Company of British Columbia established in 1889 in Vancouver. This company employed a series of small steamers for calls on the many lumber and fish camps which dotted the coastline of this great province. The company's original fleet consisted of tugs, scows, and one ferry. Down through the years combined freight and

SS CALIFORNIA. First of the gold rush steamers to arrive in San Francisco and also the first to engage in the coastal trade.

—San Francisco Maritime Museum

SS KROONLAND. *SS Kroonland,* on a world tour, shown at a San Diego wharf in 1915. The *Kroonland* at that time sailed for the Panama Pacific Line.

—*From Union Title Insurance and Trust Company Historical Collection*

passenger vessels were added and by 1922, the company possessed 14 vessels. More recently Union Steam sold out to the Northland Navigation Company of Vancouver.

Alaska was originally explored and settled by the Russians, who through the years established a series of trading posts throughout this vast region. One of the important Russian posts was located at Sitka, in Southeastern Alaska. It was here that one of the first steamboats was used by the Russians. This vessel was the *Politkofsky,* built of Alaska cedar, and started out in 1865 as a revenue cutter or gunboat. The *Politkofsky* was employed both as a warship to protect the various posts and also as a commercial vessel. When the United States purchased Alaska in 1867, the *Politkofsky* was sold with the territory. The Americans used the vessel as a tug and passenger ship. In 1897 she was converted into a barge and eight years later ended her days by piling up on the beach near Nome during a storm.

The whistle from the old steam tug *Politkofsky* has been used to signal the opening of two fairs in Seattle; namely, the 1909 Alaska-Yukon Exposition and the recent Century 21 Exposition.

One of the first steamship companies to establish a steamship service to Alaska was the pioneer Oregon concern, the North Pacific Transportation Company.

In 1867, it placed the steamers *Oriflame, Little California,* and the *John L. Stephens* on the Alaskan route, providing irregular service. During the 1880's, the Pacific Coast Steamship Company established a service from Puget Sound to Alaska. In a company folder, dated 1887, the following service was described relative to its side-wheeler steamer *Olympia:*

"She will be first class in her fittings and appointments, being furnished with electric lights and all modern appliances and improvements for the comfort and convenience of passengers . . . She is fast and will make the trip from Tacoma, Washington Territory, to Alaska and return in eleven days . . . She will connect at Victoria with the *Steamer George Elder* from San Francisco."

On July 15, 1897, there arrived in Seattle the Steamship *Portland* carrying a ton of gold. The vessel had three boxes and a large safe containing $700,000 in gold dust, all of which was carried in the captain's cabin. The mining men arriving at Seattle on the *Portland* had enough gold dust in their pokes to amount to $964,000, actually making two tons of the precious metal.

The use of the word "ton" got into the newspapers and helped dramatize the story in the eastern press. This "Quickened the pulse of venturesome men throughout the universe," drawing attention to the

SS TENYO MARU. An early day deluxe Japanese passenger liner that called at San Francisco.
—J. A. Casoly

richest gold strike in the history of the world that was made in the Klondike. One man who operated in the gold field for one winter was said to have brought out $135,000 in gold on the *Portland.*

Another gold ship, which arrived at the gold fields and first pushed her way through the ice was the *Steamer Excelsior,* which on her return to San Francisco had a similar story to tell.

Later on, the steamship history of Alaska down to almost the present day was pretty much the history of the Alaska Steamship Company of Seattle. Founded in 1895, the company started operations with a small fleet of vessels which were adapted to Alaska's Inside Passage. First of such vessels was the *Willapa,* to be joined later by the *Steamships Jefferson, Victoria, Tacoma,* to be followed later by the *Aleutian* and *Mt. McKinley.* All these vessels were combination cargo and passenger vessels. In 1954,

the Alaska Steamship Company withdrew its passenger service and now operates strictly as a freight carrier.

For a period of time prior to World War I until the late 1920's, the Pacific Steamship Company employed the passenger ships *Dorothy, Emma,* and *Ruth Alexander,* plus some Admiral Line vessels such as the *Admirals Watson, Benson,* and others in the Alaskan trade.

The rugged coastline of Alaska brought its toll of ships through the years. Both the Alaska Steam and the Pacific Steamship Company suffered heavy losses, as did the Canadian Steamship operators. The construction of lighthouses and modern navigational aids have very materially cut down the losses along its vast coastline.

Shortly after the arrival of the gold rush steamers at San Francisco, the Pacific Mail pioneered the first steamship route northward up the coast with the sailing of the *Str. Columbia* in 1850 for Astoria, Oregon. Later the company constructed a wharf at St. Helens, on the Columbia River to serve as a terminus for the line. Shortly afterward, the Pacific Mail's *Fremont* began calling at Portland, on the Willamette River, being the first coastwise ship to do so.

In the 1860's there appeared a small California steamship operation of coastal steamers which, within the next two decades grew into a giant organization. At the peak of its operations, it is said this Pacific Coast Steamship Company had vessels sailing from San Diego up the coast as far North as Alaska. Among some of the company's pioneer vessels were the *Steamships Santa Cruz, Ancon, Monterey,* and *Orizaba.*

By the time of the present century, the Pacific Coast Steamship Company withdrew from the coastal trade by selling its vessels to other steamship lines. One of these was the newly organized Pacific Steamship Company, founded by H. F. Alexander. Alexander was associated with a number of other steamship companies and operated his vessels under the Admiral Line banner. Most famous of these was the *H. F. Alexander,* known as the "Greyhound of the Pacific." The *H. F.,* originally named the *Great Northern,* was a sister ship of the *SS Northern Pacific,* and both were originally operated by the Great

"COLORADO," FIRST CHINA LINER OF PACIFIC MAIL CO.

SS COLORADO. First American steamer to sail out of San Francisco in the transpacific trade.
—*San Francisco Maritime Museum*

Northern Railroad magnate, James Hill. These were luxurious 23-knot steamers and were used by Hill on a fast run between San Francisco and Flavel, Oregon, from which point the passengers rode by rail up the Columbia to Portland. The idea was to compete for the passenger trade with the Southern Pacific Line from San Francisco to Portland.

Two other colorful coastal liners for their day were the steamships *Harvard* and *Yale.* These two 3,700-ton, former New York-Boston liners, were brought to San Francisco in 1916 and placed on the

SS MIIKE MARU. First steamer sailing to the Orient from Seattle.
—*Seattle Historical Society*

SS ORIZABA. Old Pacific Coast Steamship Company vessel employed in the coastal trade.
—*From Union Title Insurance and Trust Company Historical Collection*

run from that city to Los Angeles and San Diego. These two excursion vessels were very popular with the traveling public. They often steamed at 25 knots and were well built to ride the ground swells up and down the coast. The *Harvard* became a total loss when she ran aground at Point Arguello on the California Coast. The *Yale* was used as a barracks ship for a construction company in Alaska and was later towed to San Francisco for scrapping.

The passenger business in the coastwise trade by American vessels came virtually to an end during the depression years of the 1930's. The only passenger business today along this coast is by the vessels of foreign lines, many of whose ships make regular calls at Pacific Coast ports.

Along the coast of California and Oregon there was, in the 1870's, a lumber activity which required an unusual operation of a steamship. A series of small lumber carriers were designed for operation along these coasts to load lumber close to the shore line. Because of the relative regularity of the coastline, these ships would have to anchor off shore, or head into several small bays or "dog holes," to load their lumber. Special rigs for carrying lumber from the cliff down to the ship played a large part in the unusual loading process. In some instances a long chute was placed aboard the vessel. In others, long cables allowed the vessel to lie off shore resulting in a much safer method of loading. Other vessels were loaded with swing loads attached to an aerial from the shore out to the vessel. There was always the danger of a storm blowing up and forcing the vessel to head for sea in the midst of a loading.

The *SS Willapa,** of 752 tons, might be described as a typical lumber schooner of the period. This particular vessel was known as a "single ender" in contrast to other schooners that were "double ended." The *Willapa* was built of Douglas fir and was designed to carry a large deckload of lumber. This vessel had a poop deck and a forecastle to protect the ends of the load during the rough weather at sea. Fires and reefs ended the careers of many steam schooners along the Pacific Coast. The *Willapa* waited until she was off the coast of Honduras before going ashore and becoming a total loss in 1916.

2. TRANSPACIFIC TRADE

The first vessels to engage in the transpacific trade were believed to be the Manila Galleons, which began their operations from the port of Acapulco, Mexico to the Philippines. These sailing ships began operating under Phillip II of Spain in 1565 and lasted until 1815. Much of the cargo brought back to America from the Far East by these galleons consisted of the finest silks, satins, and crepe materials. They also carried stockings, kimonas, silk bed cov-

*Not to be confused with an early Alaskan steamer with the same name.

30

erings, tapestries, table cloths, and rich vestments for the church. Practically all of these were of Chinese craftsmanship.

Next to arrive in the Pacific from North America were the China sailing ships from Boston and nearby ports. During the voyages stops were often made at Pacific Coast ports, Hawaiian Islands, the Philippines, and westward to China. The earliest trade with China was promoted by Portuguese navigators, who had arrived from the opposite direction during the sixteenth century.

The Pacific Mail Steamship Company was the first steamship organization to establish a westward transpacific steamship service to the Orient. Steamships of the Pacific Mail dominated the transpacific trade for a number of years and remained in this service for some forty-eight years. The company's China line began with the sailing of the 3,728-ton wooden side-wheeler, the *Colorado,* from San Francisco on January 1, 1867. The departure of the *Colorado,* with her 250 "adventurous passengers," caused considerable interest and excitement along the San Francisco waterfront, as evidenced in the colorful

description appearing in the San Francisco Bulletin, "The noble steamer in her berth, the moving crowds about her and over-running her, the thronged heights, the calm blue waters of the bay, the clear prospect of the Alameda shores and the sharp outlines of the islands in the bay, altogether made a brilliant and animated scene."[1]

The *Colorado* was followed by other wooden steamships which pioneered the lengthy journey to and from the Orient. Some of these earlier vessels were the *Great Republic, China, Japan, America, Orizaba, Alaska,* and the *Dakota.*

These wooden vessels were later replaced by those of steel. In 1908, the Pacific Mail added three more ships to its transpacific fleet. The sailing schedule at this date included calls to Honolulu, Manila, and ports in Japan and China. These vessels remained in transpacific service until June, 1915 when the Pacific Mail announced that it would dissolve 67 years from the date of its establishment.

One of the most colorful steamship lines in the Pacific, if not in the world, was the fleet of the "Empress" steamers which the Canadian Pacific Railroad

SS ANCON. Companion vessel of the *Orizaba* in the early Pacific Coast trade.
—From Union Title Insurance and Trust Company Historical Collection

placed on its route between Western Canada and the Orient. The fast, trim-hulled Empress steamers, with their yellow stacks were a familiar sight on both sides of the Pacific. During its transpacific history, the Canadian Pacific Railroad saw such pioneer steamship lines as the Northern Pacific, Great Northern, and Pacific Mail gradually withdraw their vessels from the transpacific service to be followed after World War II by the Canadian Pacific itself.

Three "Empress" steamers were first placed in service by the Canadian Pacific Railroad, in 1891, and were the three finest and fastest vessels on the Pacific. They were the *Empress of India, Empress of Japan,* and *Empress of China.* These express steamers were built in 1890, expressly for the Canadian Pacific Railroad and they were the only twin-screw ships in the Pacific for some eight or nine years. Despite the limited cruising range of the older type vessels and the vast distances to be covered, "no Empress steamer missed a sailing nor was ever penalized for late arrival of the mails during the years from 1891 to 1906." The early steamers were recognizable by their clipper bows, three tapering spars, and two funnels "jauntily raked aft" that gave the yacht-like appearance. The later Empress ships were painted white with double funnels of buff, with a checkered flag in the center.

The origin and purpose of the checkered house flag of the company is interestingly expressed by the designer, William Van Horne, who states, "Yes, I designed the house flag—partly to differ from any in use and partly that it might be easily recognized when hanging loose. It has no historic or heraldic significance. Somebody suggested that it meant 'three of a kind,' but that would not be a big enough hand for the Canadian Pacific Railroad for which a 'straight flush' only would be appropriate."[2] The flag was added to the buff funnels in 1946. It was also Van Horne who chose the title "Empress" for the liners.

The Pacific Empresses served as valuable transports during the war period from 1939 to 1945. The *Empress of Japan II* was the only survivor. She was renamed the *Empress of Scotland* and after a refit in 1949, she became the flagship of the company's North Atlantic fleet.

The Canadian Pacific Railroad suffered such heavy losses during the last war, the company found it impossible to resume its Pacific service, although the "red and white checkered flag did return for a short period from August, 1952 to May, 1954" when a freight service was attempted.

The rapid extension and development of the Nippon Yusen Kaisha Steamship Line is perhaps one of the most phenomenal in maritime history. Organ-

SS WILLAPA. Pioneer vessel in the Alaska trade in the service of the Alaska Steamship Company.
—*J. A. Casoly*

SS PORTLAND. Alaska Gold Rush steamer reported to have arrived in Seattle with a "ton" of gold.
—*Seattle Historical Society*

ized in 1885, for service in Japan waters, the company within a period of ten years had begun to extend its operations on a world-wide basis. At the turn of the present century, and down to the start of World War II, the Nippon Yusen Kaisha Line's vessels were to call at ports on every continent on the globe. From the very beginning, the Nippon Yusen Kaisha, as well as other Japanese lines, received generous government subsidies for the purchase of old ships, and the construction of new ones for the nation's far flung fleets.

There were two major reasons why Hill wanted to affiliate himself with a Japanese steamship service to the Orient. Hill had brought his Great Northern Railroad to Seattle, in 1893, and it was Captain Griffiths, a pioneer steamship man of Seattle, who sold Hill on the idea of the vast trade possibilities of operating connecting steamship service to the Orient

with his railroad. The second factor, in inaugurating this service, was the desire of Hill and the Japanese to overcome a trade monopoly enjoyed by the Pacific Mail.

James Hill sent Captain Griffiths to Japan, in February, 1896, to invite the Nippon Yusen Kaisha to open a transpacific service to Seattle. Captain Griffiths returned with a deal which provided a combined freight and passenger service, whereby it would be routed over the Great Northern Railway to the Eastern United States. Seattle, in 1896, had a population of only 6,000 persons and it was apparent that the Northwest could absorb but a small fraction of trade with Japan, thus the need for rail connections to the Central and Eastern United States.

The arrival of the first Japanese steamship the *Miike Maru* was the cause of a great celebration in Seattle. The people of Seattle thronged down to the

STR. BAILEY GATZERT. Well-known and popular stern-wheeler on both the Columbia River and Puget Sound.
—*Joe Williamson*

pier where the *Miike Maru* was moored. The Seattle Times of that great day said editorially, "The hearts of the people in Seattle were in the greeting extended today to the *Miike Maru.* No more welcome craft plowed the waters of Elliott Bay . . ."

The N.Y.K. Line continued to prosper from that day on. The old vessels operating on the Seattle route were replaced, in 1901, by three English-built vessels and named the *Shinano Maru, Koga Maru,* and *Iyo Maru.* By 1904, four additional vessels of 6,000 tons were placed on the same route. The Nippon Yusen Kaisha, since its inception, had an interest in the growing shipbuilding industry of Japan, and it was not long before a majority of its ships were built in the home yards. The situation was instrumental in developing and expanding new routes throughout the world during the fifty years of the company's operation.

Incidentally, many attempts have been made to explain the meaning of the world "Maru," which is found on the names of Japanese ships. Of the several derivations of the word indicated by Braynard, the most logical one to him, is that it stood for some treasured household word connected with business. According to an early Chinese legend of some 4,000 years ago, there was a messenger by the name of Hakuda Maru who was sent to aid the people in their shipbuilding. The Japanese legend has it that "Maru" was associated with a god who lived under the sea. One can readily agree with Braynard, when he states that "its true meaning has been lost in the mists of antiquity."[3] Modern shipping men have more or less defined the word as meaning a vessel engaged in commercial trade.

While an entirely different origin of the word appears in a recent volume, "The Engine Powered Vessel," "Japanese ships received at their christening a sort of family name, 'Maru,' which, however, does not mean ship. The term is derived from the Japanese national flag, which as we know, symbolizes the red

34

H. B. KENNEDY. Fast early-day steamer generally found on the Seattle-Bremerton run.

—*Seattle Historical Society*

sunrise. The flag is called 'Hino Maru' meaning the roundness of the sun. The Japanese consider the circle to be the perfect geometrical shape. A ship at sea with its human and mechanical resources and functions is felt to be a complete organism worthy of honorary title of 'Maru.' Young men well developed from a body and soul point of view were formerly allowed to add 'Maru' to their family names. During the age of chivalry castles were also granted the right to use the title. The Emperor's palace 'Gohom Maru' is an example."[4]

By 1930, the Nippon Yusen Kaisha began to add more ships to its ever-expanding fleet. Three of her motorships, the *Tatsuta Maru, Chichibu Maru,* and the *Asama Maru,* were of the 16,975 gross tons class. The company also placed on its San Francisco-Oriental route, three cabin motorships of approximately 11,622 tons, known as the *Hiye Maru, Hikawa Maru,* and the *Herin Maru.* While many of the vessels had three smoke stacks, the Japanese shipbuilders had reasons for limiting the number of stacks on its commercial vessels. The *Chichibu Maru* carried

STR. KITSAP. Typical early-day passenger vessel of Puget Sound's "mosquito fleet."
—*Seattle Historical Society*

STR. TACOMA. Former fast Puget Sound steamer on the Seattle-Tacoma run.
—*Seattle Historical Society*

one, while the *Tatsuta* and *Asama Maru* had two stacks. The reason for this limitation is revealed in an interesting belief in Japan that "three" is an unlucky number. This was borne out several years ago when three naval vessels were built and each had three funnels. As it developed two of the naval ships met sudden disaster. The Japanese builder broke the jinx by having the third vessel fitted with two stacks instead of three.

Like many Japanese lines, the Nippon Yusen Kaisha returned in the 1950's to the high seas following the disastrous war. Also like so many other Japanese steamship operations, new and very modern cargo liners were gradually built to reenter the world trade routes.

Although Jim Hill, later known as the "Empire Builder," had started a service to the Orient with the Japanese Steamship line, he was not one to work through partnerships for very long. The coming and going of the N.Y.K. vessels to Seattle's harbor made him feel very uneasy. He decided to establish his own steamship line to the Orient, which proved to be his undoing. He ordered the construction of four huge combination cargo and passenger liners for this trade. Only two of the four were built and these were the 28,000-ton steamships *Minnesota* and *Dakota*. The two ships were placed on the Seattle-Orient run in 1905, but profits from the two liners failed to materialize. The *Dakota* ran on a submerged reef near

Yokohama in 1907 and was a total loss. The remaining vessel steadily lost money for its owner and was eventually withdrawn during the fall of 1915. The *Minnesota* was too large a vessel for this trade and was also beset with labor trouble that was beginning to brew in the American Maritime business.

One of the most phenomenal steamship growths on the Pacific Coast was that of the Dollar Steamship Company of San Francisco. The Dollar Steamship organization grew from a few lumber schooners along the California Coast to a giant world-wide fleet. No American steamship line has, perhaps, been as greatly publicized as the Dollar concern. Much of the color and publicity connected with the company's operations were centered around the activities of its founder, Captain Robert Dollar. Dollar's tall, slender frame, and goatee were a familiar sight on both sides of the Pacific. This "Dean of American shipping" has also been described as a "home-loving man whose high courage, faith and vision brought to him in the sunset years of his life the fruits of unremitting toil and honest purpose."[5]

Captain Robert Dollar was born in Falkirk, Scotland, in 1844, and at 11 years of age was working as a chore boy in a Canadian lumber camp. This Scotchman, of the Canadian and Michigan woods, came to California in 1888, where he engaged in the lumber business north of San Francisco. Later, he opened a lumber office in San Francisco and began

PRINCESS VICTORIA. Early passenger vessel in the Canadian Pacific fleet and first of the C.P.R.'s "Miniature Ocean Liners."
—*Canadian Pacific*

to charter ships to carry redwood and sugar pine logs to the United Kingdom.[6]

Dollar's first venture in the steamship business as an owner and operator, began with the purchase in 1893 of a steam schooner, *Newsboy,* a vessel 129 feet long and of only 200 tons.[7] This small vessel was used in the lumber trade along the California Coast. For his next venture, he bought a 6,500-ton steel ship, in 1901, which he named the *M. S. Dollar.* He used the vessel to carry government supplies to

the Philippines, following the Spanish-American War. This first contact with the Far East led him to undertake other ventures until he built up a tremendous steamship organization engaged in the trade between San Francisco and the Orient.

The Dollar Line vessels carried the dollar sign on their smoke stacks which was to become a familiar sight in nearly all ports of the world. Captain Dollar had used the sign as a stamp on lumber sold in his yards. The Dollar Steamship Company was formally

PRINCESS ELAINE. Another Canadian Pacific passenger ship of earlier days. Note the difference in height of funnels of the two vessels.
—*Leonard Frank*

SS PRINCESS CHARLOTTE. Early-day steamer operating out of Vancouver and Victoria.
—*Leonard Frank*

organized in 1901 and continued to operate until the late 1930's when the Dollar Steamship interests were acquired by the present-day American President Line.

Westward and southward from San Francisco and Los Angeles, in particular, saw the rapid growth of a steamship business that was to cover thousands of miles of ocean travel. To the west was founded the Matson Navigation Company of San Francisco and which answered the call to Hawaii. The call in the early days was for cargos of sugar and pineapple. The need to carry tourists came much later in the development of this steamship line.

Thus in 1882, a Captain William Matson founded the company that bears his name today. Born in Lysekil, Sweden in 1849, Matson at ten years of age went to sea as a "handy boy" and attended school between voyages.

He first sighted San Francisco at the age of 18, while on a voyage to the Pacific Coast. He left the ship in San Francisco and signed on for a voyage to Puget Sound. He later served on a schooner that carried coal from Mt. Diablo to San Francisco for the

old Spreckels sugar factory at Eighth and Brannan Streets.

"Commercially speaking that was his first taste of sugar . . . his first contact with an activity that was to be the cardinal factor in his life. Two years later he became master of a schooner. He had just turned twenty-one, and was made captain of the schooner *Mission Canal,* still engaged in transporting coal across the Bay."[8]

Captain Matson is described by his contemporaries as a "commanding figure, 'two inches short of six feet, with a barrel chest, broad shoulders and a step springy as a colt's.' It was said he could never find a crew who could keep his pace. He worked them hard but he paid and fed them well. . . . His chief interest in life was his ships, but they did not monopolize him. He had time for other business activities and for civil affairs. He was President of the San Francisco Chamber of Commerce, a member of leading clubs, and a frequent leader in public service. For a number of years, he was Consul-General of Sweden."[9]

In 1882, Captain Matson, through financial backing furnished by the Hawaiian sugar family of Claus Spreckels, bought shares in a 200-ton schooner which Matson had named the *Emma Claudina* after Mr. Spreckels' sister. Captain Matson sailed the *Emma Claudina* to Hilo on her maiden voyage, which served as the genesis of the Matson Line that was to follow. For the next three years, the little vessel carried general cargo to the Islands and returned with coconuts, hides, some tropical fruits, and increasing amounts of sugar shipments.

The first steamship to be operated by the Matson Line was the *Enterprise* and placed in Hawaiian service in 1901. This vessel was followed by a whole array of steamships down through the years, including such well-known ships as the *Lurlines I, II* and *III, Wilhelmina, Matsonia, Mololo* (Flying Fish).

In 1926 the Matson Navigation Company acquired the steamship operations of the Oceanic Steamship Company including the older vessels the *Sierra, Ventura,* and *Sonoma*. These vessels were later replaced by C-2 type freighters bearing the same names. The former passenger business performed by the *Sierra, Ventura,* and *Sonoma* was later transferred to the Matson passenger liners *Mariposa* and *Monterey* where more extensive service was provided.

The extremely long steamship route from Pacific Coast ports to the land down under; namely, Australia, and New Zealand, was first developed through a joint agreement between the Pacific Mail and the Union Steamship Company of New Zealand in 1885. This first service called for ships to touch at Hawaii, between New Zealand and San Francisco. The working agreement continued until 1900 when the Union Steamship Company was forbidden, under a new American law to trade between the newly acquired Hawaii and ports of the United States. The New Zealand company withdrew in favor of the Oceanic Steamship Company of San Francisco. The latter company was founded by John D. Spreckels, whose family had become associated with sugar interests in Hawaii for a number of years. He was the son of Claus Spreckels, the "Sugar King" of California.

The first steamships of the Oceanic Line were the 3,000-ton *Mariposa* and *Alameda*. Each made 13 trips a year over a distance of some 7,000 nautical miles. In 1900, these vessels were replaced by new 6,000-ton steamships *Sierra, Sonoma,* and *Ventura*.

Another steamship line to operate across the Pacific from the United States to Hawaii was the American-Hawaiian Line. Instead of working out from San Francisco, this company's operations were based in New York. This company first sailed around the Horn to Hawaii with square-rigged and clipper ships. These sailing vessels would call at San Francisco, where the sugar was transferred to railroads for delivery to East Coast refineries. The need for a faster more regular schedule called for the establishment of a steamship line, in 1900, carrying sugar from Hawaii around the Horn to the East Coast. Four 8,000-ton steamships, the *American, Hawaiian, Californian,* and *Oregonian,* were placed in this service. All the American-Hawaiian steamship or cargo vessels from that time on employed the suffix "an" or "ian" to the end of the ship's name. As the years progressed the company's fleet grew larger in number and size.

As a combined transpacific and intercoastal oper-

SS PRINCE RUPERT. Early popular Grand Trunk Railway's liner employed on the Vancouver-Seattle run.
—*Clinton Betz*

STR. NEWSBOY. First vessel to be owned and operated by Capt. Robert Dollar, founder of the Dollar Steamship Company of San Francisco.   —*American President Line*

ation, the company had an interesting history.

First, the American-Hawaiian went around the Horn and up through the Straits of Magellan and then continued its voyage to Hawaii. This, of course, proved to be a slow and costly route. So the next method to shorten its travel was to use the Isthmus of Tehuantepec where the cargo was transhipped across the Isthmus to vessels on the Atlantic and Pacific sides. This was carried out between 1907 and 1914, when the Panama Canal was opened for business.

In 1923, the headquarters were transferred from New York to San Francisco. The company continued to prosper until 1953 when it withdrew from the

steamship trade. High labor costs, Panama Canal tolls, and other features caused it to cease operations. This company in very recent times is considering re-entry in this trade with a container-type service, which is so popular today.

The opening of the Panama Canal served as a boon to American and European shipping. The American phase was represented by an intercoastal trade that flourished for some fifty years. Besides the American-Hawaiian Line, which used the Canal for its East Coast sugar shipments, there was the Luckenbach Steamship Company of New York, whose freighters were a common sight on the West Coast until 1962, when it withdrew from this trade.

With the opening of the Canal in 1914, the Luckenbach's *SS Pleiades* was the first commercial vessel to make the transit. This vessel was followed through the years by the construction of large freighters. Most of such carriers bore the name of a member of the New York shipping family such as the steamship *Andrea Luckenbach, Lewis Luckenbach,* and others. Conditions in the intercoastal trade involving high labor costs, and competition with American railroads forced the Luckenbach operations to shut down in 1962.

Another American steamship company to pioneer a coastal and intercoastal route to the Pacific Coast was the W. R. Grace & Co. of New York. A year after the opening of the Canal in 1914, four "Santa" steam-ships ranging from 7,000 to 10,000 tons were placed on the run from New York to San Pedro, San Francisco, Portland, and Seattle. These vessels were the *Santa Clara, Santa Catalina, Santa Cecelia,* and *Santa Cruz.* Later Grace Line ships were operated between Pacific Coast ports to ports on both coasts of South America. This latter service prevails today and their freighters have accommodations for a limited number of passengers.

The Canal opened up trade to other lines, both American and European, and which still flourish today. Vessels from nearly all over Europe bring manufactured goods, paper, and fertilizer in exchange for Pacific Coast apples, citrus fruits, and lumber products.

STEAM SCHOONER EVERETT. Typical lumber carrier engaged in the early steam schooner operations along the Pacific Coast.   —*Steamship Historical Society of America, Inc.*

SS ALASKAN. Early-day American-Hawaiian Steamship Company vessel.
—*From Union Title Insurance and Trust Company Historical Collection*

SS ENTERPRISE. One of the first steamers in the Matson Company fleet.
—*Matson Navigation Co.*

SS MONGOLIA. Pacific Mail Steamer in the transpacific trade about 1903.

—Steamship Historical Society of America, Inc.

SS SIBERIA. Another member of the Pacific Mail fleet of early days. The markings are to identify the ship during World War I. *—J. A. Casoly*

SS H. F. ALEXANDER ex GREAT NORTHERN. Fast coastal passenger liner that ran from San Francisco to Puget Sound ports.
—*Steamship Historical Society of America, Inc.*

SS ZEALANDIA. Early Pacific Mail passenger liner on the Australian run. Photo taken about 1875.
—*Steamship Historical Society of America, Inc.*

SS EMPRESS OF JAPAN. One of the famous "Empress" vessels of the 1930's. She was the second vessel in the
C.P.R. fleet to use this name.
—*Leonard Frank*

SS SIERRA. First Oceanic Steamship Company vessel and the first ship to bear this name.
—*Oceanic Steamship Co.*

SS PRESIDENT COOLIDGE. One of the later Dollar Line vessels in the transpacific trade. Notice the Dollar Sign on the stacks.

—Dollar Steamship Co.

SS AORANGI. Former Union Steam vessel employed on the long Vancouver-New Zealand and Australia run.

—Union Steamship Company of New Zealand

SS CATALA. Early member of the fleet operated by the Union Steamship Company of British Columbia for travel in B. C. waters.

—Clinton Betz

SS ADMIRAL WATSON. One of the Admiral Line vessels of the former Pacific Steamship Company.
—*Clinton Betz*

SS NORTH COAST. A freighter belonging to the former Northland Transportation Company of Seattle.
—*Clinton Betz*

SS ALASKA. A typical passenger liner of the Alaska Steamship Company fleet in the 1920's.
—*Steamship Historical Society of America, Inc.*

SS NORTHWESTERN. Pioneer Alaska Steamship Company vessel. She had many close calls in Alaskan waters but came out without any serious damage.
—*Clinton Betz*

SS YALE. Sister ship of the *SS Harvard*. Both steamships were very popular with the traveling public between San Francisco and Southern California.

—*Matson Navigation Company*

CAPTAIN WILLIAM MATSON (1848-1917). Founder of the Matson Navigation of San Francisco, which company is still a major shipper in the trade with Hawaii.

—*Matson Navigation Company*

SS AVALON. Well-known steamer on the passenger run between Los Angeles and Catalina Island.
—*Steamship Historical Society of America, Inc.*

SS MENESTHEUS. A British Blue Funnel Line vessel commonly seen for years in Pacific Coast ports. This line adopted Greek names for its vessels.
—*J. A. Casoly*

SS CATALINA. Companion vessel to the *Avalon*.
—*Steamship Historical Society of America, Inc.*

SS OHIAN. An American-Hawaiian vessel of a later period.
—*J. A. Casoly*

SS PAUL LUCKENBACH. One of the Luckenbach Steamship Line vessels when it was engaged in the former inter-coastal trade.

                            —J. A. Casoly

TUG NEPTUNE. A San Francisco based steam tug, large enough for both bay and deep sea towing. Most tugboats today have converted from steam to Diesel power.

                            —J. A. Casoly

SS LONE STAR STATE. This belongs to a company that operates in a world-wide steamship service. The company's ships calling along the Pacific Coast are generally in the transpacific trade.

—*States Marine Lines*

SS IROQUOIS. A former Great Lakes steamer brought to Puget Sound for a passenger service out of Seattle.
—*Steamship Historical Society of America, Inc.*

MV IROQUOIS. The same vessel converted into a Diesel freighter on Puget Sound for the Black Ball Line.
—*Black Ball Freight Service*

MV COQUITLAM. The *Coquitlam* was formerly a member of the coastal fleet of the Union Steamship Company of B. C. located at Vancouver.

—Leonard Frank Photos

Chapter III

Ferries of Yesterday and Today...

WHENEVER AND WHEREVER BOATS of all descriptions have been built, they frequently have been used to ferry people, or cargo, across some body of water. The body of water was perhaps more often an important crossing point such as a stream or river. Ferries have also been used to cross bays, inlets, and lakes.

The history of ferrying along the Pacific Coast shows a variety of crossings. In San Diego, there developed a short ferry crossing from that city to Coronado. San Francisco Bay was the scene of a most lively ferryboat trade for nearly one hundred years. Ferrying was a common practice on such rivers as the Sacramento, Columbia, Willamette, Snake, Fraser and others. The waters of Puget Sound and British Columbia very early witnessed a vast ferrying service which operates to this day.

1. SAN FRANCISCO BAY

Ferryboat travel on San Francisco Bay followed various routes throughout the bay area. Most of these began at the terminal clock tower at the foot of Market Street in San Francisco to such places as Oakland and Alameda to the east, to Sausalito in Marin County, and Richmond and Vallejo at the upper end of the Bay. The Northern part of the Bay also had some shorter ferry routes such as the one from Point Quentin, near San Rafael to a point near the town of Richmond. Even the town of Vallejo had a short ferry route to carry workers across the narrow channel to the Naval Yard at Mare Island. Farther up the Bay at the mouth of the Sacramento River, at an area known as Carquinez Straits were two ferry services which now have been superseded by bridges. One was a train ferry used by the Southern Pacific Railroad to ferry trains across the Straits from Port Costa to a place near Benicia across the river. Farther up stream was a passenger and later a small car ferry between the towns of Martinez and Benicia.

The operation of a ferry service across San Francisco Bay probably began in 1850 when a Captain Thomas Gray offered transportation from San Francisco to Oakland with his screw steamer *Kangaroo*. This service first began with a twice-a-week schedule. The original purpose of Gray's ferry service was to provide the "excursionists a trip 'across the Bay' and an opportunity to visit the wondrous region of Contra Costa."[1]

The Trustees of Oakland created a public authority three years later in which a daily service was to be provided between Oakland and San Francisco. For approximately the next 100 years the railroads have interested themselves in some form of ferryboat operation on the Bay. The chief purpose being to transport train passengers and some freight between the East Bay and San Francisco, or between the Marin shore and San Francisco.

FERRY ALAMEDA (1). First ferry to be named for the City of Alameda. This ferry was built for the old San Francisco and Alameda Railroad in 1866.

—J. A. Casoly

The first of these railroads was the Central Pacific, a predecessor to the Southern Pacific of today. The Central Pacific had extended its line in 1869 from the old terminus at Sacramento to what was then a terminus at Alameda. Train passengers were now ferried from the Alameda Pier to San Francisco's Davis Street Wharf. Shortly after the Central Pacific transferred its Alameda terminus to Oakland where it remained in operation until the ending of ferry service in 1958. This terminus became to be known as the "Oakland Mole."

Several East Bay cities began in 1905 to be served by electric trains some of which were merged in conjunction with the Sacramento Northern electric line as a feeder for passenger service for commuters traveling between the East Bay and San Francisco. From these mergers grew the Key Route System which operated its own ferry system. The Key Route ferries followed a route from its terminus near the Oakland Mole along the southern shore of Yerba Buena Island and on to its pier in San Francisco.

At the turn of the century, the Santa Fe Railroad began operating a ferry service from its Richmond terminus to San Francisco. A British Columbia steamer *Ocean Wave* was brought down from New Westminster, B. C. for the service.

When the Western Pacific had reached the East Bay it too offered a ferry service from its pier on the Oakland side of the Estuary for the transportation of passengers and freight to San Francisco. The fast stern-wheeler *Telephone* was brought down from the Pacific Northwest for this service.

FERRY ALAMEDA (2). This Southern Pacific ferry built of steel in 1913 was operated up to the cessation of ferry operations on the Bay. She was also one of a few ferries on the Bay to have two funnels. —*J. A. Casoly*

In 1907, the Northwestern Pacific Railroad started a ferry service from Sausalito and Tiburon in Marin County to San Francisco. This provided a passenger service across the Golden Gate for not only these ports in Marin County, but for passengers who were to board the train for points between Sausalito, Tiburon, and Eureka. In the early 1920's a competitor appeared on this ferry route in the form of an automobile ferry. The automobile by now had come into its own and new ferryboats were being built for this new lucrative traffic. Auto ferry service between Marin County and San Francisco saw the establishment of the Golden Gate Ferry Company which had built a ferry slip at the foot of Hyde Street in San Francisco. The Southern Pacific also engaged in an auto ferry service from the East Bay to San Francisco. In 1929, the Southern Pacific entered into a joint operation with the Golden Gate Ferry Company

and the Northwestern Pacific Railroad whose ferry service remained in this operation until such traffic came to an end with the building of the Golden Gate Bridge. The building of the San Francisco-Oakland Bay Bridge, about the same time, began to cut into auto traffic between the East Bay and San Francisco.

The type of propulsion showed an interesting transition through the years. The earlier ferries were steam driven employing paddle wheels at the stern or on the side of the vessel, the latter being referred to as a side-wheeler. Later, some of the ferries changed over to the screw propeller and employed this type to the very end. The later Key System ferries were powered by a single screw, but it was turned by two electric motors from a steam turbine. This provided for an unusually smooth ride in contrast to the other ferries in the area. Many earlier ferries and most of the

60

river boats used stern wheels, no doubt, due to the narrow channels along the route.

Where paddle wheels were used, the walking beam assembly could be seen protruding above the top deck as the vessels passed. The working of this huge beam is interestingly described in Harlan and Fisher's book, "Of Walking Beams and Paddle Wheels." "For the casual observer, the engine room held a spell of fascination, while for the habitual commuter whose 'very own' seat was on the lower deck, the engine room was literally a shrine. When the last express cart had been towed aboard and the milling crowd had found favorite seats on the familiar benches after the last train had disgorged its human contribution to the ferry's load, the engineer, attired in his blue serge uniform, put down the magazine he had borrowed from the newsstand, ducked down the metal stairs into the polished chambers that were the capitol of his domain, and grabbed the glistening bar which had been worn smooth by the hands of generations of ferry engineers before him. Slowly he began to raise and lower the bar, causing the paddles to slowly churn seafroth against a quivering ferry slip

so that the deckhands could unhook the huge hawsers from the sides of the slip. Then suddenly the picture changed as the telegraph's bell clattered madly, the big hand on the annunciator dial swung wildly back and forward, finally coming to rest on 'Full Speed Ahead'—then for the engineer it was down bar—up bar—down again—up—down for one last time, and with a clattering of metal the reverse lever was thrown into place, the eccentrics came crashing down onto the now-revolving camshaft and the engineer wiped his hands on a handful of waste, looking up at the admiring audience with a quiet air of pride in a job well done—and while the engineer hooked up his starting bar, the fascinated spectator looked out upon the Bay to find to his surprise that the pier had been cleared several minutes before and that the boat was under way."[2]

The peak year for passenger and automobile ferry operation in the Bay Region was in the year 1930. From that time on the need for ferry passenger transportation began to lessen. In 1933 the Western Pacific and Santa Fe arranged for the Southern Pacific to carry their train passengers. The completion of the

FERRY BERKELEY. The ferry Berkeley was the first ferryboat with a screw propeller drive and was of steel construction.
                                                                                          —J. A. Casoly

BERKELEY INTERIOR. Ornate interior of the ferry Berkeley. Even the wooden seats carried a pattern at the back.
—*J. A. Casoly*

Bay and Golden Gate bridges in 1939 spelled doom to the ferry which gradually shut down operations. In 1939 East Bay commuters were using the electric trains on the San Francisco Bridge. The Key Route System's ferries *San Leandro* and *Hayward* continued to carry passengers to the Golden Gate International Fair on Treasure Island in 1939 and 1940. The Southern Pacific still ran on a limited schedule as train ferries between San Francisco and the railroad terminus at the Oakland Mole until 1958.

2. PUGET SOUND FERRIES

Ferry operation on Puget Sound and British Columbia waters shows an interesting development with respect to two types of ferryboats. Because of rather lengthy routes to various ports of the Sound and in the British Columbia area, steamers were first used for commuter travel, instead of the typical, short, broad-beamed passenger or auto ferries as we know today. On Puget Sound it was the "mosquito fleet" that performed the ferrying service to the various parts of the Sound. There were a few exceptions such as the ferry *Seattle* that ran a short distance between Seattle and West Seattle in the early days. These small passenger steamers served the cities, the resorts, the small towns, and sawmill ports alike. The Puget Sound steamers were operated for several years by the Puget Sound Navigation Company, successors to the Kitsap Transportation Company, and the Black Ball Line.

In 1951 the car ferries began to appear on the

scene and they ranged in capacity from 6 to 100 automobiles. The ferryboats, in the Washington State System at the present include the 52-year-old former side-wheeler *Leschi* and 10 San Francisco ferries, nine of which were given Indian names. For example, the San Francisco ferry *Lake Tahoe* became the *Illahee* and the ferry *Stockton* was named the *Klickitat.* The *San Mateo,* the last active steam ferry on the Pacific Coast is being retired by the Washington State Ferry System. The *San Mateo* has remained in the fleet with very little alteration. Built in 1922, she was in her day one of the nation's largest car ferries. It is possible that she may be given a place of honor in some Maritime Museum.

As of 1965, the Washington State Ferry System was using 26 ferries on 13 all-year routes connecting Western Washington highways with 13 islands, the Kitsap and Olympic Peninsulas, and Vancouver Island. The state ferry system has plans for new and larger ferries that will carry 2,000 passengers and 160 vehicles compared to 1,140 passengers and 100 vehicles under the present fleet. There has been plenty of evidence that the investment will be a sound one, even as a tourist attraction, which at the moment seems to have unlimited possibilities. Also, more people are living outside of the large cities and the ferry is one of the best ways of commuting.

A brochure published by the Washington State Ferry System relates: "As a tourist attraction, the Washington State Ferries has much to offer. At present, the fleet consists of 24 vessels, largest in the United States. These ferries travel approximately 2,500 miles daily during the peak summer season. Tourists can visit such places as the beautiful San Juan Islands, the rugged Olympic Peninsula, and old-world Vancouver Island via the most scenic marine routes in the world. Since May, 1966 tourists have been able to extend their ferry travel beyond the bounds of Washington State Ferries by connecting with the Canadian and Alaskan Ferry Systems."[3]

Thus the "salt water highways of Puget Sound" afforded by the ferries have a bright future in the years to come, providing this beautiful body of water is not spanned by a series of bridges.

3. BRITISH COLUMBIA FERRIES

As was indicated at the beginning of this chapter, the early ferry operation in British Columbia waters was by fairly large steamers owned first by the Canadian Pacific Railroad, and to a limited extent by the Canadian National Railroad, both transcontinental railroads of Canada. The C.P.R., being the largest operator, employed a series of "Princess" vessels in the various ports of Southern British Columbia waters.

J. D. PETERS. This ferry ran from San Francisco to Stockton via the San Joaquin River. She operated in this service from about 1900 to 1918 when she was relieved by more modern riverboats. —*J. A. Casoly*

FERRY SAN LEANDRO. This ferry was originally built for the Key System in 1923 and was purchased later by the Southern Pacific.   —*J. A. Casoly*

The main routes to various points of the Georgian Straits, and to Vancouver Island from the City of Vancouver included the popular run from Vancouver to Victoria, Vancouver to Nanaimo and from Vancouver up the coast of the mainland and to various islands lying off Vancouver Island. Another popular route was from Vancouver to Seattle, either direct or via Victoria and return. Many of these early passenger ferries were three-stackers, as was the case of *Princesses Victoria, Charlotte, Elaine,* and *Elizabeth.* In 1949 the C.P.R. brought out two sister ships, the *Princess Marguerite* and *Princess Patricia.* The *Marguerite* has a straight raked stem, cruiser stern, and carries two funnels and two masts. She has accommodations for 2,000 day passengers, and sleeping accommodations for about 100. The sister ship *Patri-*

cia has recently been used cruising to Alaska, while the *Marguerite* has been placed exclusively on the run between Victoria and Seattle.

Previously, it has been noted that a series of "Prince" passenger vessels competed with the C.P.R. for commuter travel out of Vancouver. These steamers were originally operated by the Grand Trunk Pacific Steamship Company of Vancouver and included such steamers as the *"Princes"* George and *Rupert.* These ships were built especially for the British Columbia and Alaskan service and also were placed on the Vancouver-Seattle run. The *Prince Rupert,* sister ship of the early-day *Prince George,* was a three-stacker and had accommodations for 200 first-class passengers. There is a war story concerning the *Prince Rupert.* It seems that the German

FERRY TAMALPAIS (2). This ferry operated between San Francisco and Sausalito across the Golden Gate to a terminal at Sausalito.

—*J. A. Casoly*

Cruiser *Dresden* in 1915 was about to shell the British Columbia Coast when the *Prince Rupert* showed up upon the horizon. The Germans mistaking the vessel's three funnels for a British warship, quickly withdrew from the scene.

The Canadian National Railroad absorbed the Grand Trunk in 1921 when the former company confined its operations to voyages to the town of Prince Rupert and Alaskan ports. Recently this company has employed a new deluxe *Prince George* for this trade.

When the demand for vehicle traffic became more apparent, the C.P.R. made an effort to engage in this service. Like the early Puget Sound steamers, the C.P.R. tried to convert a few of their "Princess" ships to this trade. It served the purpose at the beginning until automobile and truck traffic worked a hardship on the vessel. The chief difficulty was that passenger liners with their relatively narrow beams could not hold many cars at a time. Instead of loading through a wide mouth at one end, the cars had to be loaded through the side of the vessel and often lowered to the deck by means of an elevator. Later on specially built ferries were built to provide ease in loading. Out of this need appeared a specially constructed vessel like the Black Ball Line's *MV Coho,* which incidentally loads from a side near the bow. The Canadian Pacific brought out two modern ferries, the *Princess of Nanaimo* and the *Princess of Vancouver* and they were placed on the Vancouver-Nanaimo run.

About 1960 a Premier of British Columbia, by the name of W. A. C. Bennett, conceived the idea of a state-owned ferry system. Starting with a ferry operation between Tsawwassen, near the City of Vancouver, and Swartz Bay on Vancouver Island, Bennett has today created one of the world's largest ferry

FERRY REDWOOD EMPIRE. Early ferry operated between San Francisco and the Marin Shore by the Northwestern Pacific Railroad. Later on it became a member of the Golden Gate Ferry System fleet.

—*J. A. Casoly*

FERRY YERBA BUENA. This ferry was a sister ship of the Peralta and the second Key Route ferry to bear the name of Yerba Buena. The vessel shown on this page was built in 1927 in Oakland. She was scrapped in the 1950's after serving in the Army Transport Service during World War II.

—*J. A. Casoly*

EARLY AUTO FERRY. Picture of one of the first automobile ferries. The cars and trucks were parked in the center of the boat allowing room on the sides for the movement of the passengers.

—*J. A. Casoly*

FERRY DELTA KING. The sternwheeler Delta King, a sister ship of the Delta Queen. These were actually river boats on the run between San Francisco and Sacramento. The Delta King was later used as a barrack ship for a mining company in British Columbia. The Delta Queen is operating as a cruise ship on the Mississippi River.

—J. A. Casoly

operations with 23 vessels and 19 terminals. His latest addition was to place a new *Queen of Prince Rupert* on the run between Kelsey Bay, at the northern end of Vancouver Island, to Prince Rupert, where passengers and their cars may continue to Alaska on the Alaska-owned ferry system.

Besides the Vancouver to Victoria run (Tsawwassen-Swartz Bay) the British Columbia Ferry Authority has ferries on a route between Vancouver (Horseshoe Bay) and Nanaimo, up the Sunshine Coast, Saltery Bay, Bowen Island, Vancouver and the Gulf Islands. All these routes have about covered all the important ferry routes of the previous operators. Competition between the new ferry authority and the C.P.R. has forced the latter to dispose of the 18-knot ferry *Princess of Nanaimo*, which was sold in 1963 to shipping interests in Nova Scotia.

Mention was made earlier of the Black Ball Line's ferry *Coho*. This vessel was placed on the run between Port Angeles and Victoria in 1959. The Amer-ican-owned Black Ball Line had a modern ferry *Chinook* on the Nanaimo run, but no longer operates this service. This vessel was sold to the British Columbia Ferry Authority in 1961.

4. ALASKA STATE FERRIES SYSTEM

When the Alaska Steamship Company gave up its passenger business following World War II, it left a dire need for a passenger service by water. The Alaskans were beginning to depend more and more on air travel and as a consequence became quite air-minded. However, air travel could not build a highway system which is sorely needed in this vast state. Plans were made to operate a car ferry along the Southeastern Coast from Prince Rupert in British Columbia to Skagway.

Thus in 1963 a new state-owned ferry system was established with the sailing of the *Motorship Malaspina*. She was soon followed by the *Motorships Matanuska* and *Taku*. All three vessels were named for Alaskan glaciers. These ferries are capable of

FERRY CHINOOK. Streamlined ferry built in 1947 for Black Ball Line and later sold to Canadian ferry interests.
—*Seattle Historical Society*

carrying 100, or so, automobiles, or 50 large trailers, and 500 passengers. There are a few sleeping accommodations for the passengers. The vessels are 352 feet long, with a beam of 74 feet and a speed of 18 knots. The ferries are modern in every respect, being equipped with the latest electronic navigational aids.

The ferries sail from Prince Rupert and head northwest along the famous Inside Passage, with the first stop at Ketchikan, Alaska. From there the ferry makes calls at Wrangell, Petersburg, Sitka, Juneau, and Skagway. The ferry route is 624 miles shorter than by the present automobile highway.

5. ASTORIA-MEGLER FERRY

About 1921 the automobile had become an important means of travel and there being no connections between Astoria in Oregon and across the mouth of the Columbia River to the Washington side, a Swedish carpenter living in Astoria decided to build a passenger and car ferry. Thus the *Motorship Tour-* *ist I* started a service under the name of the Astoria-North Beach Ferry Company. The *Tourist* had a capacity for 16 cars. Three years later (1924), car ferry *Tourist II* was placed on this service and had a carrying capacity of 23 autos. In 1931 a third *Tourist* was placed on this run. Following World War II, a steel ferry, *Motorship M. R. Chessman,* was built at

FERRY KALAKALA. Former Key System Peralta and reconverted into this streamlined vessel for use on Puget Sound by the Washington State Ferry System.

—*Seattle Historical Society*

FERRY KLAHOWYA. Like most of the ferries in the Washington State Ferry System, they have Indian names for their vessels.

—*Joe Williamson*

Portland with a capacity of 44 cars. By 1962 Puget Sound ferry *Kitsap* was purchased for the five-mile crossing.

Auto and truck traffic increased rapidly through the years and finally the highway authorities decided to construct a high level bridge across the body of water. The bridge was formally opened in the early fall of 1966 and the ferries were withdrawn from this trade.

FERRY TILLIKUM. Another modern ferry in the Washington State Ferry System.

—*Joe Williamson*

MV HYAK. One of the latest vessels to be entered into the service of the Washington State Ferry System. The HYAK was the first of four super ferries to be built for Puget Sound service. The new vessels will be larger and faster than those now in operation. They will be able to carry 60 per cent more automobiles and have 30 per cent more speed.

—Washington State Ferry System

FERRY COHO. This Black Ball Line ferry is named for a species of highly prized salmon. The vessel does double duty during a 24-hour period each day. By day she operates as an auto ferry between Port Angeles, Washington and Victoria, B. C. By night the Coho serves as a freighter between Seattle and Puget Sound ports.

—Black Ball Line

SS PRINCE GEORGE. Coastal steamer *Prince George,* first of the name by the Canadian National Railroad. This photo was taken about 1919.
                                                                        —*Leonard Frank Photos*

SS PRINCE GEORGE. Modern Canadian National liner engaged in the Vancouver to Alaska trade and is a very popular tourist vessel. This is the second ship to bear the name *"Prince George."*
                                                                        —*Canadian National Steamships Photo*

MV QUEEN OF BURNABY. Modern British Columbia Ferry System vessel which is presently on the run between Tsawwassen near Vancouver and Swartz Bay on Vancouver Island for auto and passenger service to Victoria.

—Commercial Illustrators, Ltd.

MV QUEEN OF NANAIMO. This vessel is presently on the run between Horseshoe Bay near the City of Vancouver to Nanaimo on Vancouver Island.

—British Columbia Government Photo

QUEEN OF THE ISLANDS. This aptly named ferry is used for service among the islands off the southeastern coast of Vancouver Island.

—*British Columbia Government*

POWELL RIVER QUEEN. Especially designed vessel for limited traffic and short runs.

—*Commercial Illustrators, Ltd.*

QUEEN OF PRINCE RUPERT. One of the latest British Columbia ferries and which had the honor of inaugurating a new service between Kelsey Bay, on Vancouver Island, and Prince Rupert on the mainland. This new route has offered travel by water from Vancouver or Victoria to the port of Prince Rupert.   —*British Columbia Ferries*

PRINCESS OF VANCOUVER. A modern Canadian Pacific ferry used on the Vancouver-Nanaimo run. She is shown passing under the Lions' Gate Bridge.   —*Canadian Pacific Railway*

MV MALASPINA. A close-up view of one the popular Alaska ferries.
—*Glenn Long*

MV TAKU. Another member of the Alaska ferry fleet named for an Alaskan glacier.
—*Joe Williamson*

Chapter IV

Steamship Disasters at Sea...

THE COASTLINE FROM SAN DIEGO to Alaska has been in the past a virtual graveyard for both ships under sail and steam alike. Shipwrecks along this far-flung coast were due to many causes. Some were the result of an uncharted coastline, scarcity of lighthouses and other navigational aids, storms, fog, and strong currents made such sailing a hazard. The loss of a steamship in the Aleutian Islands of Alaska as late as 1965 makes the danger of shipwrecks still a real hazard today. Even the more navigable river systems along the coast with their unmarked shoals and bars caused many a riverboat to go ashore in the early days.

Other disasters on water were man made. Failure to heed navigational warnings. Taking a chance against tides and other errors resulted in many costly wrecks. Fire on board ship was still another hazard of the sea.

One of the perils of early-day steamboating, according to Norman Hacking, was the danger from explosion. In his article, "Steamboats on the Fraser in the 'Sixties,' " Hacking states that "boilers were often of flimsy construction, inspections were inadequate, and ambitious captains had a lamentable habit of holding down the safety valve when tempted to race speedier vessels. As a consequence the western rivers of North America had an appalling record of bloody disasters."[1]

In this chapter a brief description will be made of a few disasters which have occurred to steamships along the Pacific Coast. The various other accounts, now in book form, have described the fate of vessels during the past 100 years.

As might be expected, daring rescues both off shore and out at sea were made innumerable times. The wonderful work of the U. S. Coast Guard through the years is well known. Rescues at sea by merchant vessels is a common practice. The Maritime Administration of the United States Department of Commerce issues the coveted Gallant Ship Award to those ships that engage in a rescue at sea. The Gallant Ship Award is a bronze medallion depicting a ship steaming full speed ahead with a bronze plate to describe the action for which the award was presented. Not long ago, the American Mail Line's *Philippine Mail,* of Seattle, engaged in a rescue of the Chinese vessel *Hai Ziang* off the northern tip of Formosa. The vessel was found listing 45 degrees to the port. Cold northerly winds had whipped up a heavy sea 12 feet high. The skipper, in this situation, maneuvered his vessel to the windward of the *Hai Ziang* and pumped oil overboard to smooth the rough sea. A volunteer crew of eight set out for the stricken ship. Five persons jumped overboard, of which three were immediately saved, and the other two found later lashed together were saved by two

GALLANT SHIP MEDAL. A medal that is given to ship's officers and the crew for heroism and bravery in going to the aid of a stricken vessel.

—*Marine Digest*

crewmen from the *Philippine Mail*. The *USS Weiss* hove to about this time and she placed her power whaleboat in the water and removed the remaining men on board the stricken vessel. The medal for this heroic effort was awarded as follows: "The courage, resourcefulness, expert seamanship, and teamwork of her master, officers, and crew in successfully effecting the rescue of nine persons from a sinking ship under extremely hazardous circumstances have caused the name of the *Philippine Mail* to be perpetuated as a Gallant Ship."[2]

1. YANKEE BLADE

During the gold rush days steamers were sailing up the coast from Panama and Nicaragua to the port of San Francisco where the prospective miners headed inland to the gold fields. As a consequence, several steamships were wrecked along this extensive route. Many of these vessels became total wrecks and experienced a large loss of lives. Others were more fortunate in getting off with minor loss.

One of these more fortunate wrecks was the one in which the steamer *Yankee Blade* piled up on the shore at Point Arguello, 15 miles north of Point Con-

ception, on the California Coast in 1854. It seemed that the Captain of the *Yankee Blade* missed his reckoning and steamed full speed through a dense fog onto the beach. Her bow ploughed 60 feet up on the beach, while her stern remained in 9 fathoms of water. It was not very long before the deck houses on the stern were washed away. Boats, of course, were lowered and the process of landing passengers ashore was partially successful in the daylight hours. There was panic aboard and some of the passengers jumped into the sea. It was said that the captain showed his cowardice by being one of the first ones to go ashore in the ship's boats. Fortunately, the *Str. Goliath* from San Francisco came upon the vessel and rescued most of the passengers. Out of some 700 passengers only 15 lost their lives, a record much better than most shipwrecks on this coast.

2. STR. PACIFIC

One of the worst wrecks along the Pacific Coast occurred on November 4, 1875 when the *Str. Pacific* collided with the *Str. Orpheus* off Cape Flattery near the entrance to Puget Sound. In this collision, out of 275 persons aboard the *Pacific,* only one survived.

The *Pacific,* equipped with side-wheels and sails, had cleared the Port of Victoria, B. C. and was headed out to sea through a mist and was passing Cape Flattery about 9:00 p.m. when the passengers and crew felt a terrific shock. The quartermaster, being thrown from his bunk, stated later he thought the vessel had struck a rock. The collision between the two vessels smashed a deep hole in the bow and forecastle of the *Pacific* and rapidly filled with water. Men and women, in their night attire, hurried on deck and began to struggle for a place in the lifeboats which later proved to be unseaworthy. The ship next began to list sharply and many were thrown into the water. The quartermaster said he was saved by a hatch cover and he was later picked up by a Coast Guard cutter. The other vessel, the *Orpheus,* went aground the next day on Vancouver Island.

3. THE ISLANDER

As noted before, the rugged coast of Alaska proved to be a graveyard for many early-day vessels. Many sank within a short period of time, others survived to allow a rescue of passengers and crew, and still others ran high on the ledges, or rocks, and were fortunate to escape serious damage and be refloated again. Vessels belonging to the Canadian Pacific Steamship Company and to the American Alaska Steamship Company were lost in both the Inside Passage and Northwestern Alaska.

One of the several C.P.R. vessels to become wrecked in Alaskan waters was the 1,495-ton *Islander.* Here was a steel, twin-screw steamer that was ideally built for the British Columbia trade. On the evening of August 14, 1901, the *Islander* left Skagway at the head of the Inside Passage and sailed through floating ice in Stephens Passage. Despite the ice, the captain did not reduce the speed of the ship. About 2:15 a.m. the vessel suddenly struck a low-lying iceberg. The shock of the blow put a strain on the ship's wooden superstructure causing the stateroom doors to jam. The chief officer said afterwards it was like hitting a boom of drifting logs. The captain could not now steer the vessel and within a few brief moments the *Islander* began to sink at the bow with the rudder lifted clear out of the water.

Panic occurred on board ship and the slanting of the decks made it clear that the vessel was sinking. Passengers and the crew were roused from their sleep, but it was too late to reach many of them. It was later estimated that the *Islander* went to the bottom within 18 to 20 minutes. Of the 172 persons aboard (109 passengers and a crew of 63) forty were never accounted for, including the captain who obviously went down with his ship.

Since many of the passengers had boarded the ship from the Klondike gold fields, it is believed that some $3,000,000 in gold went down with the ship. The vessel was raised 30 years later and the amount

SS PACIFIC. Only one person survived among 275 passengers when the Pacific was lost near Cape Flattery in 1895.
—*San Francisco Maritime Museum*

NEIL O'HENLY
of Uist, Scotland.
Aged 21 Years
Quartermaster S.S. Pacific

Lost Nov 4 1895
Near Cape Flattery
Only Survivor of
275 Passengers and Crew

SS VALENCIA. The Valencia struck rocks on Vancouver Island in 1906 with a large loss of life.
—*Seattle Historical Society*

of gold that was recovered only amounted to $40,000.

Of the several "Princess" ships that met their fate in northern waters, two are described here, the *SS Princess Sophia* and the *SS Princess Kathleen.*

4. PRINCESS SOPHIA

Sailing through a blinding snow storm caused the *Princess Sophia* to become stranded on Vanderbilt Reef, also near Skagway. There were 345 persons aboard, including 218 men, 35 women, 17 children, and 75 members of the crew. The *Princess Sophia* left Skagway at 10:00 p.m. en route to Vancouver, B. C. on October 24, 1918 when she ran aground, 40 miles from Juneau, at 3:00 in the morning. A number of passengers were thrown out of their bunks and great excitement took place. Boats were not made ready when the information was received that the vessel was not taking water. This news quieted the passengers and no boats were lowered. The Captain in the meantime had wirelessed his home office to the

effect that the ship was in no immediate danger, and also the vessel had a double bottom. Snow continued to fall and a northwest wind blew up. The next morning no passengers were taken off because of the heavy seas. A lighthouse tender came near the wreck and stood by to give aid. Somewhere between 8:00 p.m. and 7:00 a.m. the following morning the vessel had slipped off the reef and sank carrying 345 persons to their deaths.

The last message from the ill-fated *Sophia* read, "For God's sake come! We are sinking." A terse wireless message afterwards from the lighthouse tender *Cedar* to Juneau read, *"Sophia* driven over reef during night. Only masts showing. No survivors. Blowing storm. Started snowing this morning. *King* and *Wing* assisting."[3]

Investigation later showed that the *Princess Sophia* had been turned around by the heavy seas and the bow could no longer hold the vessel in position and she slipped down the smooth rock into the sea.

82

5. PRINCESS KATHLEEN

Also near Juneau, the *Princess Kathleen,* the "Queen of the Alaska liners," crashed ashore on a high ledge on the Alaska mainland at 3:00 a.m. in 1958. She crashed with 328 aboard near the site of the ill-fated *Princess Sophia* 34 years before. According to one of the survivors a violent shock and a frightening sound of torn metal was heard. Men and women were thrown out of their bunks and rushed to the deck in complete confusion. Word was given to abandon ship. One by one the passengers and the crew went over the side and down the ladder to the rocky beach below. The passengers, it developed, lost all their baggage and personal belongings. The incoming tide floated the ship but she filled up fast, and like the *Sophia,* she slipped off the ledge into 90 feet of water after having remained on her perch for some 12 hours. Fortunately no lives were lost, but the company lost a 4 million dollar vessel.

6. RIO DE JANEIRO

The San Francisco Golden Gate has for many years been the scene of numerous wrecks. The entrance to San Francisco Bay is often beset by either fog or strong tides which have been a factor in many a wreck. There is another factor, that of negligence on the part of the ship's officers. As one early-day mariner declared, "The most frequent cause of shipwreck on this coast (Pacific) is the neglect of taking soundings in thick foggy weather . . .".

Such was the case in the wreck of the Pacific Mail Line's *Rio de Janeiro.* This developed to be one of the strangest disasters in early-day shipping. On the morning of February 21, 1901, the *Rio* was anchored in the Golden Gate about 3½ miles from where she went down. The captain ordered the ship to weigh anchor at 4:00 a.m. and the vessel proceeded on a N. E. course at a speed of about eight or nine miles per hour. The weather at this time was clear, but shortly afterwards the fog rolled in enveloping the entire vessel. No one aboard knew the exact position of the ship as apparently no soundings were made. Suddenly there was a crash and the vessel struck a rock and she sank almost immediately in 50 fathoms of water taking 131 victims with her.

The people on land could hear the vessel's distress signal through the fog, but could not locate her. The pilot of the vessel claimed afterward that his vessel was on course all the time, that it was the strong current that sent the vessel on the rocks. The *Rio* is thought to have struck a ledge of rock at Fort Point, which is near the anchorage for the present-day Golden Gate Bridge.

Only 82 of the passengers and crew were later

SS GOVERNOR. Pacific Coast Steamship Governor was destroyed by fire off the coast of Washington.
—From Union Title Insurance & Trust Company Historical Collection

SS SOPHIA. Went to her doom in the icy waters of Southeastern Alaska. She slipped off a reef and sank with 345 persons aboard.
—Marine Digest

rescued by small boats. A San Francisco newspaper the next day explained the catastrophe by stating that the suction of the sinking vessel drew some to their death, while others who were able to secure safety on the wreckage were too exhausted to call for aid.[4] Mail bags with valuables floated to the surface and were broken open by "ghouls who always flock to the scene of disaster." First news of the tragedy came to the attention of a marine reporter who had been standing on San Francisco's Meiggs Wharf. He saw a lifeboat coming out of the mist with thinly clad people on it. He next saw the name of the lifeboat and then he knew that the *Rio* had been wrecked.

7. SS GOVERNOR

Another early morning disaster occurred when the popular passenger liner *SS Governor,* of the Admiral Line, was struck by the freighter *West Hartland* which took place in April, 1921. The collision occurred near Port Townsend, near the entrance to Puget Sound, at 12:04 a.m. At 1:15 a.m. the *Governor* sank carrying eight persons with her. It was the biggest tragedy to strike the Northwest at that time.

At the time of the accident the *Governor* carried 113 passengers and a crew of 124. The vessel was en route from San Francisco to Seattle at the time and was only a few hours steaming time from her wharf at Seattle. Rescuers, shortly after the collision, ran along the decks smashing windows to arouse those sleeping in the various staterooms as the *Governor* went down. She took a big list and it looked for a while that it might keel over and strike one of the lifeboats carrying the last two men from the stricken vessel—the captain and the wireless operator. The vessel's stern rose in the air and she began to break in two. Quick and heroic work by rescuers prevented a larger loss of life.

8. SS VALENCIA

The *SS Valencia* went ashore in January, 1906 between Bonilla Point and Cape Beale, the very area where a number of ships had ended their career in years gone by. The reason this area had been dangerous to navigation is interestingly stated: "And not knowing the exact set and strength of the currents, a shipmaster might never be sure of his charge until the roar of the breakers against the Vancouver Island shore gave him a warning of the close approach. Lucky was the sailing craft if it could then work off the dreaded lea-shore into healthy sea room....Most of the time they could work free. Occasionally they were caught, though, as in the case of the *Valencia* which proved to be the most terrible sea-tragedy ever chalked up against the 'Graveyard.' "*

* See Footnotes for this chapter.

"A combination of circumstances contributed to build up the dreaded reputation of this area. Even when all is plain sailing, the navigator of a ship coming up from the south doesn't open the Strait of Juan de Fuca until his vessel is miles beyond Cape Flattery; and the same applies to the vessel coming from the Northwest along the great circle from the Orient. The Coast of Vancouver Island, running in the same direction as the mainland coast of America, looks like a combination of it from any distance. It fooled Captain Cook; he sailed right by because there was no apparent break in the coastline."*

"A vessel under certain circumstances such as inability during foggy weather or stormy weather to 'shoot' the sun, might overrun the estimated distance from point of departure to point desired."*

The *Valencia's* officers not hearing the surf resulted in the vessel crashing against a rugged promontory or cliff on the shore. The ship not only became a total loss, but the drowning of nearly all of her passengers (145) including many women and children made it one of the worst sea disasters in this area. The ship was 10 miles off her course and it was the first voyage in this area for the vessel's master. Because of the severe weather conditions, the *Valencia* had passed a possible rescue ship, the *SS Queen City*.

The *Valencia* could not have landed in a worse place for rescue work. When rescuers reached the ship 40 hours later, a heavy sea had completely destroyed the boathouse and washed hopeful passengers

* See Footnotes for this chapter.

out to sea. The passengers in their long wait tried to keep up their courage by singing "Nearer My God To Thee." One of the crewmen tried to swim ashore with a line, but failed because of the high cliff on the shore. Incidentally he was the one who got away on a raft and lived to be awarded an honor from the President of the United States.

Living near the scene of the wreck were the Daykin boys who reported about four o'clock in the afternoon, while one of them was working on the telephone lines, someone kept breaking in and finally a voice exclaimed, "There's been a shipwreck and for God's sake send some assistance." Daykin estimated the call had come from a lineman's shack up the shore. Later it turned out to be the party appealing for help was a Seattle high school teacher by the name of Bunker and who had managed to reach shore, the only survivor in his lifeboat.

One other member of the lifeboat got ashore, but later lost his life trying to get his family ashore. Only a handful survived the worst wreck along the Pacific Coast.

9. SS KENKOKU MARU

An unusual story of the salvage operations necessary to refloat a vessel is shown by the plight of the *SS Kenkoku Maru* after she ran ashore in a dense fog 70 miles north of San Francisco. The *Kenkoku Maru* had previously led a stormy life, having been bombed during the final attacks on Japan. She was rebuilt in 1950, and then piled up on the beach in California a year later. Tugs and barges were immediately sent

PRINCESS KATHLEEN. Photo of the Princess Kathleen before her fatal disaster in Alaskan waters.
—*Clinton Betz*

WRECK OF THE PRINCESS KATHLEEN. The vessel slid to the bottom of this ledge.
—*U. S. Coast Guard Photo*

to the scene, but gale winds prevented salvage operations until the fifth day of the beaching of the vessel. Heavy gear was also set up on shore to aid the tug to move the vessel. The plan was to move the ship both astern and asea. The idea being that the combined power of the barge was to be pulled seaward, the ship's winches also to be pulled seaward against anchored tackle, and shore equipment to be pulled astern.

On the ninth day there was an eastern movement of 90 feet followed by further movement the next two days. Then there was a waiting period for the high tides of 10 to 13 days. On the 20th day a movement of 100 feet was accomplished and on the 25th day since being stranded, the vessel was finally pulled into deep water. She was then towed to a drydock at Alameda for repairs. There was also a problem of drydocking the vessel because no one was sure how strong her hull might be. "The diver found that the bottom of the vessel was touching the keel blocks for only a few feet fore and aft and that amidship the vessel was unsupported. To correct this condition the diver spent many hours carefully tacking up the keel blocks to provide sound support for the vessel along her keel and he also inserted wedges wherever necessary between the bilge blocks and the vessel's corrugated bottom. When the keel block tacking and the bilge block wedging had been completed, the task of raising her gently began."[5]

Other problems developed in placing the vessel in drydock for the necessary repairs. The workers in the drydock worked around the clock to slowly raise the vessel enough to provide a dry dock underneath. When this was finally accomplished, repairs to the ship's plates were made. The inspectors found that only a few of the plates in the vessel's entire bottom could be salvaged. The vessel was eventually repaired. Considered by many to be a complete loss, the salvage and repairs were considered to be a "nine day wonder" on the West Coast.

Sometimes a vessel does not have to be at sea to meet disaster. Ships have been known to sink, or burn, at wharves.

In Seattle in 1933 an American Mail liner capsized at her dock carrying five men to their death. The vessel keeled over shortly after 5:00 p.m. with the stern of the ship finally resting on the bottom while the bow remained out of the water at a 60 degree angle.

In the meantime there was an elderly storekeeper who was asleep when the vessel sank. It was 10 hours later before he was rescued from his "watery grave."

"I died ten times during the night," exclaimed the 61-year-old seaman, "but I came to life each time."

The storekeeper had quit work about 5:00 p.m. and had climbed into his bunk for a snooze when the ship started to capsize.

"The water came in with a rush and everything

was rolling around, banging and falling down. I decided the only thing to do was to sit tight and wait for her to go down. The motion finally stopped, however, so I knew everything was all right. By midnight I went to sleep. I woke up at dawn but decided there wasn't anything to do except to wait for them to come and get me, so I went back to sleep," he added.[6]

Two Chinese who had been trapped in the ship's pantry room were pulled to safety through a porthole after they had made their way up from the interior of the vessel.

SS KENKOKU MARU. The Kenkoku Maru is shown here hard aground off the California Coast. After many days of salvage work she was refloated and towed to a dry dock. *—Marine Engineering and Log*

Chapter V

Some Unusual Steamships and Motorships...

WHAT CAN BE UNUSUAL about a ship? For one thing, it could be a matter of size, speed, or long life. A ship may also be different from others because of a special type of cargo it carries. And, again it may be the unusual way in which a vessel carries its cargo. The following are a few examples of these different kinds of ships and their handling requirements.

1. SIZE

In a previous chapter it was mentioned that James Hill, builder of the Great Northern Railroad, had invited the Japanese to offer a steamship service to Seattle. This man later decided to operate his own steamship line to the Orient. In 1905, as was stated in Chapter II, he ordered the construction of four huge cargo-passenger liners, of which only two were built. These were the *SS Minnesota* and the *SS Dakota*. And for their day, they were the largest American vessels to operate in the Pacific. In fact they were the largest American vessels touching our shores including the Atlantic Ocean.

In order to see how big these ships really were, an examination of the *SS Minnesota* will attest to its size for the time when it came into operation. She measured 630 feet in length, and 72 feet in width and had a gross tonnage of 28,000. The *Minnesota* had eleven decks and accommodations for 50 first-class, 100 second-class, and 1,000 steerage passengers. But these figures do not necessarily represent bigness. It was her holds or hatches that were so large. It is said that they could swallow a complete locomotive. If you placed the *Minnesota* in the center of a big city street, she would extend up to the seventh story window of a building.

Her sister ship, the *Dakota,* ran ashore and sank in Japanese waters in 1907. The *Minnesota* was sold in 1915 to new owners on the East Coast. When the huge vessel left Seattle she carried the largest load for a ship in her time. It is said that some of her cargo was suspended from her masts!

2. SPEED

Of the many ocean-going vessels calling at Pacific Coast ports, mention should be made of two passenger liners which were not only speedy vessels, but were also known for their beautiful lines. One of these was the *SS Great Northern* later named the *H. F. Alexander.* The *Great Northern* and her sister ship the *Northern Pacific* were brought to the Pacific Coast and placed on the run between San Francisco and a port near the mouth of the Columbia River, where its passengers would board a train to Portland. These sleek narrow-hulled vessels made their journey in twenty-five to twenty-six hours and by doing so offered serious competition to the Southern Pacific's crack Shasta Limited from

San Francisco to Portland. The *H. F.* was built for speed and could, if necessary, move through the water at 25 knots. Because of her speed she was known as the "Greyhound of the Pacific." During her life at sea she broke all kinds of records for speed. To mention a few, in 1916 she made the fastest trip by a merchant ship from San Francisco to Honolulu in three days, 19 hours, and 57 minutes. Until 1939, she held the record in the Atlantic for the fastest round trip voyage between New York and Europe. Because of her speed she proved to be a crack troop ship for the American forces during both World Wars and she needed no convoy like the slower vessels.

Late in the last century, the Canadian Pacific Railroad had finished a line from Montreal to Vancouver. Shortly afterwards the railroad established a steamship line to the Orient with fast vessels to bring back tea and valuable silk from China and Japan. For this service the steamship company built a series of beautiful passenger-cargo liners and were known the world over for their speed. These vessels bore the name of "Empress" and were easily recognized by their white hulls, buff-colored funnels and yacht-like sterns. The rounded stern gave the ships the appearance of speed which they certainly had. These ships were large vessels for their day (1914). They were 16,000 gross tons, 570 feet in length, and were driven through the water by quadruple-screw propellers at a speed of over 19 knots. In 1914, the *Empress of Asia* lowered the record across the Pacific to Victoria in 9 days, 2 hours, at an average speed of 19.19 knots. In the 1920's the Canadian Pacific Railroad brought out the *Empress of Russia* and the *Empress of Canada*. The *Empress of Canada* was 625 feet long and had a gross tonnage of 21,517. She lowered the *Empress of Asia's* record a full day in 1931.

SS MINNESOTA. The largest cargo vessel in the American merchant marine in her day. Her hatches could swallow a locomotive. This picture shows the steamship taking on passengers in Seattle in the early 1900's for a voyage to the Orient.

—*Seattle Historical Society*

3. RELIABILITY

Ships are often like people. They can be very temperamental and not perform too well at sea. Others have been very dependable and often had long lives. To show how many ships may react in a reliable way, let us observe the performance of two famous ships in the Pacific Northwest. One of these was the Puget Sound steamer *Flyer*. The other was the venerable and sturdy *SS Victoria* which ran to Alaska for many years from Seattle.

The *Flyer* was built in Portland, Oregon in 1891 and was transferred to Seattle where she was rebuilt after a fire at her wharf. She was placed on the passenger run between Seattle and Tacoma which was 40 miles to the south on Puget Sound. The authors of the book "Pacific Steamboats" had something to say about this reliable, staunch little vessel.

". . . the *Flyer* set a new standard for reliability and speed as she knifed her way back and forth between Tacoma and Seattle, four round trips a day at a steady 18 miles per hour. Citizens of the two cities set their watches by the shrill whistle blast of the racing *Flyer* and her advertising slogan, "Fly on the *Flyer"* became a household phrase in the Pacific Northwest."

The authors of this same book quote a story in the Seattle Times to the effect, "With unvarying precision the *Flyer* has completed four trips daily between the two Puget Sound cities, month in and month out, traveling 80 miles to a trip and 240 miles a day, with an average of 340 working days in a year. . . . Seattle undoubtedly may claim to the possession of the most remarkable passenger steamboat in the world. The vessel is the *Flyer* plying between Seattle and Tacoma, which in the past 16 years has made the equivalent to five trips from the earth to the moon, or 51 voyages around the world at its greatest circumference."[1] The *Flyer* was retired in 1911, thus ending a wonderful career lasting some 20 years.

The second reliable steamship was the *Victoria ex Parthia*. This plain-looking but famous little vessel was very popular with early-day Alaskans and Seattleites. She was the first vessel for many years to reach Nome in the Bering Sea each spring.

Originally named the *Parthia,* she was built in Scotland in 1870. What probably gave her long life was the fact that her hull was made of hand-wrought Swedish iron measuring an inch and a quarter in thickness. This enabled her to break the ice each spring on her way to Nome from Seattle. She first served for 15 uneventful years in the Atlantic except for one year as a crack troop ship for the British in 1881. During the summer of 1887, she was brought out to the Pacific where she was placed on the run

SS H. F. ALEXANDER. The graceful H. F. Alexander is seen here backing out from her berth ready to sail on one of her voyages up the coast from San Francisco. Note the unfinished San Francisco-Oakland Bay Bridge and two of the auto ferries that were so popular on the Bay.

—*J. Casoly*

SS EMPRESS OF ASIA. Notice the yacht-like stern on this famous "Empress" ship as she steams out of Vancouver on her way to the Orient.

—Leonard Frank

from Victoria to the Orient. In 1904 her name was changed to *Victoria* and remained so until her retirement. In this year she entered the Alaskan service and remained in that trade until her retirement in 1946, thus ending a career at sea that lasted some 75 years!

This "great grandmother of Alaskan shipping" has not been forgotten. The old *Parthia* name plate, which for many years was to be found in the engine room of the *Victoria,* was transferred in 1948 to the new Cunard Liner, *Parthia.* The *Victoria's* bell is now the cherished property of the Seattle Historical Society. And her beloved whistle whose "deep vibrant voice still echoes along Alaska's rocky Coast, piercing fog and snow, announcing arrivals and departures," has been handed down to the Alaska Steamship Company's Steamship *Ilianna.* Not many other ships of olden days have lived so long.

There was an old time U. S. revenue cutter *Bear,* which although not a merchant vessel, had a most colorful and interesting career in the history of our navy.

The *Bear* came to the Pacific Coast and was operated by the U. S. Coast Guard. It was her custom to start out each spring with a load of mail, food, clothing and other necessities to the white man and Eskimo in the far north. While on her annual tour of duty,

the crew of the *Bear* would be called upon to perform many duties. It may at one time be ferrying a herd of reindeer from Siberia to feed Alaskan Eskimos, go to the rescue of an Arctic whaler, or police the beach area where the 1896 gold rush took place.

Built in 1874, the venerable old ship, of which Admiral Richard Byrd said, "ice could never beat her," sank off Nova Scotia in 1963 when she lost her tow line. The *Bear* listed badly and got water in her seams and the gallant old timer "died in actions she had lived for most of her 89 years."

4. SPECIAL DUTY VESSELS

Because of the very nature of cargo requirements of certain trade routes it is often necessary to build ships for this particular kind of service in order to obtain greater efficiency of operation. This applies to such cargos as bananas, oil, cement, lumber, automobiles and other specialized products.

Most of the bananas we eat are raised in Central or South America. This type of fruit is picked green and shipped to ports either on the Atlantic or Pacific Coast. Most of the bananas have for several years been carried by the ships of the "Great White Fleet" the vessels of which sail under the banner of the United Fruit Company of Boston. These steamships are easily recognized by their white hulls and superstructure. And by their funnels painted yellow or buff at the bottom, then a red band with a large white diamond and finally a band of black at the top of the funnel.

Bananas, being a perishable fruit, have to be handled carefully. Thus banana boats have fully ventilated holds specially built for carrying this type of fruit. The old days of handling banana stems by hand have been pretty much replaced by special conveyor belts which safely load or unload the now boxed bananas from the ship. So efficient are these conveyor belts that more than ten carloads of bananas can be unloaded in an hour.

Ever since ships have been used to carry cargo, it has been customary to load a vessel by means of booms hooked up in various ways to the mast. These booms were used to lift cargo from the dock and lower it into the hold of the vessel. This method is still used on most cargo vessels today. However, a few years ago, someone figured out that considerable time could be saved in loading and unloading if a truck van could be driven on or off the vessel without touching the contents of the van. This is known as roll-on/roll-off or trailership. The trucks are thus driven onto the

vessel at the stern very much like some types of automobile ferries.

The next step forward was to lift the van off the truck and to lower it into the hold, or fasten it to the deck. This type of loading required specially built ships and are known as container ships. Several steamship lines today are either reconverting their present vessels or building new ones for this speedy means of handling cargo. In order to load or unload the vans specially built cranes are a necessity as a part of the ship in order to lift cargos of this weight.

Older freighters began to be reconditioned into container type vessels. Briefly stated, "The holds of the vessel were paved smooth so that fork lifts could be used. New masts were engineered to lift the huge vans. Pilot houses were lifted so that pilots could see over the containers on the deck. New generators were installed to provide power for refrigeration and heater equipment."[2]

In 1966, the Sea-Land Company ordered the construction of six carriers with a capacity of over 1,200 containers, 338 reefer and 923 dry cargo containers. These container ships have a speed of 27.2 knots and

SS VICTORIA. This venerable vessel had one of the longest lives on the sea having operated for over 70 years. This was the vessel which was the first to arrive at Nome, Alaska each spring.
—*Clinton Betz*

STR. FLYER. People were said to have set their clocks to the whistle of this dependable Puget Sound steamer as she left on her daily run between Seattle and Tacoma.
—Seattle Historical Society

are 905 feet long. About the same time, the various Japanese lines announced a huge container program for their fleet.

All this led to another labor-saving idea for handling cargo known as a trainship. Here the roll-on and roll-off principle is used and instead of trucks the complete railroad car is actually loaded. This requires a specially built vessel which can load enough freight cars to make it pay. The *Trainship Alaska* is a good example of this type of carrier. The *Alaska* is a 520-foot vessel and has an operating speed of 18 knots. From 50 to 56 railroad cars, depending on their length, can be shunted on the rails to the main deck. When the main deck is full, an elevator can drop ten or eleven more cars to a lower level. Power jacks and chain buckles are used to secure each railroad car when the vessel rolls in heavy seas.

There are several advantages of a trainship. The railroad cars are protected by enclosed decks which prevent them from corrosion by salt water while on the sea. Also the cargo can be kept at an even temperature throughout the voyage.

Some vessels in recent years have been built for the carriage of automobiles for export. This case in particular began with Volkswagens being brought to the United States by a special cargo carrier. Recently the Japanese motorship *Oppama Maru* arrived on the West Coast with 1,016 Datsun automobiles. The

Oppama Maru is 500 feet long and 70 feet wide and can carry 1,200 automobiles. To make the voyage a more profitable one, this motorship loaded 16,500 tons of wheat at Portland destined for the Orient on the return voyage.

A special loading process for loading and unloading wood chips has been invented, which is similar to that of loading grain on board a vessel. A spout with a blower system is used for loading or unloading a bulk steamship carrier or barge.

A new type of cargo ship was launched recently and placed into service by the Holland-America Line as shown by the *MV Moerdyk*. Instead of having the superstructure or housing and engines in the center of the ship, they have been moved aft to allow more efficient loading and unloading operation. This provides five large hatches forward and one aft to speed up this service. The *Moerdyk* is especially suitable for the European-Pacific Coast trade. This vessel has no passenger accommodations being strictly a cargo vessel.

There is a Norwegian vessel, the *MS Rondegan*, that operates on the Pacific Coast from the paper mill at Ocean Falls to California. She is specially built to carry rolls of paper, or newsprint. On the deck are three gantry-type cranes and they are so hinged that they can reach over the ship's side in one long overreach. The paper cargo is lifted vertically out of the hold in one big grab. The load is then carried horizontally along the gantry arm and then dropped vertically onto a flatcar or hopper. This operation greatly reduces the amount of human labor. Several large rolls can be grabbed at a time. A translucent cover over the cranes protects cargo in bad weather.

Vessels carrying liquid or bulk have been with us for many years. These specially built ships are called tankers. They carry oil, gasoline, chemicals, and even wine, tallow, and molasses. On the return voyages some of them carry other bulk such as grain or rice. What does one do with a shipload of molasses? Most of it is used for livestock feeding on their mash in pellet form or mixed with grain.

Most of the tankers are recognized first by their length and also by the fact that the superstructure, housing, and engines are to be found near the stern. However, on some of the very large tankers there is an additional housing up front to provide better vision in steering the vessel.

As the years go by it seems that tankers are getting larger and larger. Some of the early-day tankers had 10,000 to 40,000 tons deadweight, but now there are some tankers of over 100,000 tons. One of these is the American supertanker *Manhattan,* the largest under our flag and the fourth largest in the world. This tanker is 108,590 deadweight tons, 940.5 feet long and has a beam width of 132.6 feet (too wide for it to go through the Panama Canal). Not long ago this huge vessel traveled up the Columbia River to load 91,000 tons of grain for Pakistan.

Tankers, too, are ships and they have to be protected from the hazards of a voyage as well as any freighter or passenger liner. The following is an interesting account of the departure of a typical "Tanker to Norway" from the "Aramco World," a recent issue.

"For the most of the day and all of the night the tanker had been loading petroleum. Hour after hour, from the great steel tanks on the hill 6,000 feet away, crude oil from the fields of Saudi Arabia had

U. S. CUTTER BEAR. Although not a merchant ship, this famous vessel rendered many years of faithful service to shipping in the Bering Sea and Arctic Ocean.   —*Official U. S. Coast Guard Photograph*

STR. GUALALA. Sea anchors and mooring lines keep this vessel in position off the California Coast in order to load lumber in the small bay.
—*The Skipper*

poured aboard, gurgling quietly through the long green mains into the dark cavities that stretch between bridge and forecastle. Hour after hour the high-riding hull had settled more deeply into the water.

"Now, at dawn, it was time to prepare for sea. The rubber loading hoses were uncoupled from the manifold; the steel cables and heavy nylon hawsers were winched in and stowed; the second of two massive bow anchors was dragged dripping from the water. A moment later the ship began to move, the stern pivoting toward shore, the bow toward the open sea. Black smoke belched from the twin stacks on the funnel deck and three shattering blasts from the whistle banged hoarsely against the purple hills of Sidon. The ship, steady on a heading of 277 degrees, steamed west across the Mediterranean. Her name was the *Esso Den Haag.* Her destination was Norway.

"There is a definite rhythm to a sea voyage. It begins on a note of excitement, levels off to a placid monotony, rises and falls with the approach of other ships, or with the advent of storms and fog, climbs to a peak in a moment of challenge and then, one

evening, or one morning, as the outline of a harbor takes shape on a distant horizon, subsides.

"Aboard the *Den Haag* the excitement was short-lived. The crew coiled lines, cleared the clutter from the deck and disappeared, leaving the decks deserted and silent. The Chief Steward, shivering in the numbing zero-degree cold of a galley freezer, chose the meat for the evening meal. The Chief Engineer checked pressure readings of instruments for an indication of some flaw he suspected in the turbine. The Second Officer took over the watch, and Captain Huibert Jansen retired to his cabin to pack his pipe and talk. The sun was warm, the sea blue and all, for the moment, was well.

"It will probably be a calm voyage," said Captain Jansen. "It usually is, this time of the year, and we have made this trip before, many times. But at sea," he shrugged expressively, "at sea, you never know."

"He gestured with his pipe toward the starboard side of the ship. 'Down there on the poop deck there's a gap in the rail and there's a ladder lashed to the railings nearby. The gap is where the ladder used to be. It is quarter-inch steel, that ladder, but when we started taking green water aboard in the South Atlantic one day it tore like a strip of cardboard.'

"The captain's words were a gentle reminder that if oil is the central fact aboard a tanker, it is not the only fact. A tanker is also a ship and Captain Jansen made it abundantly clear that once the last hose was disconnected and the last valve closed, it was to the ship and the long voyage ahead that he would give his full and undivided attention."[3]

Like railroad cars, logs have for many years been carried on scows under the tow of powerful tugs. In earlier days, logs were most often tied in huge booms like a raft and towed to their destination. Both of these methods were suitable for short distances along the coast but for deep sea or ocean travel more reliable and faster means had to be adopted. So now a new type of vessel has been built just to carry logs.

One of such carriers, the *Silver Shelton,* is a single decker ship with the superstructure and engines installed in the stern like a tanker. This leaves room for the automated loading and unloading into the fore part of the vessel. A series of cranes are used for this purpose and the logs are stowed in the wide-mouthed hatches like any other cargo. The *Silver Shelton* can carry about 5.6 million board feet per trip. Some log carriers often carry grain or some other commodity on the return voyage.

Instead of shipping cut lumber, many vessels have been built recently to carry logs. Some of these log carriers have oversized hatches located in pairs along the deck capable of accommodating sling loads of logs easily. Three oversized cargo booms, which can handle 15 tons each, also are a vital part of the log loading, or unloading equipment.

Since we live more or less in a frozen food age and we import perishable food from abroad, refrigerated ships are commonly called "reefers." Some vessels are completely refrigerated, while others are partly so. Most of this kind of cargo is essentially meat and fruits. For example, we import meat from Argentina and Australia and ship apples and citrus fruits to other parts of the world. Usually this type of vessel is divided into compartments, insulated so that they can be kept at fixed temperatures, one temperature at 15 degrees below Fahrenheit for meat, another temperature from 32-34 degrees Fahrenheit for fruits, vegetables, and dairy products.

Until recently, there was a ship on the San Francisco Bay that was designed to carry a cargo of eggs. This unusual stern-wheeler was the *Petaluma* and it was her custom to travel between San Francisco and Petaluma, a big egg-producing area in the state. The ship had a ventilated deck for the purpose of carrying this perishable product. These were the days before refrigeration on ships. The *Petaluma* gave into refrigerated cargo-vans after 33 years of travel to Petaluma. Every night it pulled out of a San Francisco pier and headed up the Bay where it entered the Petaluma slough, where it twisted and turned with 80 miles of course for 36 miles to its dock in Petaluma. The *Petaluma* had a big superstructure, and a little keel which allowed her to navigate the waters of the slough. Incidentally, the *Str. Petaluma* was the last stern-wheeler to appear on San Francisco Bay.

SS SAN JUAN. Fully loaded container vessel operated by the Sea-Land Service, Inc. and is a frequent caller at Pacific Coast ports.
—Mike McGarvey

CONTAINER SHIP LOADING PROCESS. A view of an elongated wharf showing two container vessels loading huge vans from the truck to the ship by means of tremendous cranes.
                                                            —Sea-Land Service Co.

MATSON MARSHALLING YARD IN HAWAII. Air view of huge marshalling or assembling yard for truck vans for the Hawaiian area.

—Matson Line

SS HAWAIIAN MONARCH. A reconverted vessel for container cargo shown off Diamond Head as she steams into Honolulu harbor.
Matson Line

SS ESPARTA. One of the many beautiful "banana boats" in the United Fruit Company's fleet.
—Mike McGarvey

SS CHENA. A reconverted Alaska Steamship cargo vessel for the transportation of containers is seen heading out of Seattle's Elliott Bay for Alaska.

—*Alaska Steamship Co.*

TRAINSHIP ALASKA. View showing railroad freight cars being loaded at the vessel's stern.
—*Alaska Trainship Corporation*

TRAINSHIP ALASKA. A side view of the Trainship Alaska showing her long lines and two parallel funnels.
—*Alaska Trainship Corporation*

HYDRO-TRAIN. Another method of hauling freight cars for long distance or deep water travel.
—*Puget Sound Freight Lines*

HYDRO-TRAIN UNDER TOW. This type of barge carrier is presently being used to carry railroad cars to British Columbia and Alaskan ports where railroads are to be found.
—*Puget Sound Freight Lines*

MV MOERDYK. A modern freighter which is designed to have its housing and engine room towards the stern allowing easier loading and unloading from the cargo hatches located towards the center and front of the vessel.
—Holland-America Line

MS TAI PING. A Norwegian vessel with an oriental name engaged in the transpacific trade for the Barber Line.
—Mike McGarvey

LOG LOADING PROCESS. A Japanese transpacific "K" vessel being loaded with logs by cranes from a cut down log carrier. These loading scenes occurred at Grays Harbor, Washington.
—*Seattle Stevedore Company*

ANOTHER VIEW OF SAME LOADING. The Japanese, in particular, have recently been carrying logs instead of cut lumber. This requires the vessel to be equipped with special type holds for log cargoes.

—Seattle Stevedore Company

SS MOBILE BRILLIANT. A deck view of a modern tanker while she is moving through the water.
—*Socony Oil Company*

SS MANHATTAN. Largest American-owned tanker passing through the Dardanelles en route to Odessa on the Black Sea.
—*Manhattan Tankers, Inc.*

ESSO DEN HAAG. Close view of a powerful foam spreading unit on an oil tanker to be used in fighting fire.

—*Arabian American Oil Co.*

KELP VESSEL. A highly specialized vessel designed to collect and carry a cargo of kelp. This sea weed is to be found in large amounts along our coasts. It is used for medicinal purposes.

—*Albina Engine & Machine Works*

STR. PETALUMA. This riverboat was specially designed to carry a cargo of eggs between Petaluma and San Francisco.

—J. A. Casoly

BARBARA C. These vessels were small to allow them to load lumber in various "dog holes" or small bays along the coast.

—J. A. Casoly

TUG HAROLD A. JONES. A modern day tug about to be launched in Vancouver's harbor. Note the three other tugs aiding in the launching where there is not too wide an area of water.   —*Vancouver Tug Boat Co., Ltd.*

RIVER TUG. The City of Portland's tugboat used on the Willamette River for the movement of barges and ships. She is being replaced by a Diesel tug.   —*Port of Portland Commission*

ISLAND EXPORTER. View of a huge barge shaped like a ship being towed by Victoria's Island Tug & Barge Company's Sudbury II.

—Island Tug & Barge, Ltd.

BARGE NO. 10. An unusually large barge some 300 feet long, the length of a football field, is used primarily to haul petroleum products.

—United Transportation Co.

Chapter VI

Steamships and Motorships of Today...

STEAMSHIPS AND MOTORSHIPS have called at Pacific Coast ports from all over the world. Vessels representing every continent are to be found loading at Pacific Coast ports for distant lands.

The distribution of American and foreign flag vessels along the Pacific Coast of North America shows an interesting development. An examination of a marine journal, as late as 1965, in San Francisco, revealed that there were approximately 47 steamship lines serving San Francisco and Oakland. Of these, 34 were foreign steamship lines and 13 were American-owned lines. Among the 34 foreign lines, 24 represented European countries, 7 from Japan, and 3 from India and the Philippines.

The European lines were mostly of British and Scandinavian ownership, both areas being old-timers in the sea-faring trades. Much of the European trade came to the Pacific Coast after the opening of the Panama Canal. The European vessels came out to our coast to unload manufactured goods and paper and to carry back our apples, citrus fruits, and grain. American steamship operators on the Pacific Coast, on the other hand, have besides engaging in the intercoastal trade, also followed trade routes across the Pacific and down to Australia and even around the world. Visitation by Japanese vessels started at the turn of the century and they have actively traded on our shores ever since except for the period during World War II.

Passenger business by American vessels has largely been transpacific in nature. The old passenger trade by American vessels along American ports on this coast disappeared during the depression. The same thing resulted in the intercoastal trade. Nearly all passenger business to the Pacific Coast today is conducted by vessels under European flags.

An attempt is made in this chapter to show the story of present-day steamship and motorship travel by means of pictures of representative lines among the Pacific Coast ports. Most of the vessels shown are quite modern, while a few others date back to World War II, or shortly before.

PRESIDENT ROOSEVELT. A reconverted passenger liner in the round-the-world trade for the American President Lines.

—*American President Lines*

PRESIDENT WILSON. A round-the-world passenger-cargo liner in the American President Line fleet. All vessels of the President Line are named after former U. S. Presidents. —*American President Lines*

SS CANADA MAIL. A modern cargo-passenger liner in the American Mail Line fleet engaged in the transpacific trade.

—American Mail Lines

SS DINTELDYK. Well-known visitor to the Pacific Coast in the European trade.
—*Holland-America Line*

SS MARIPOSA. Well-known and popular sister ship of the Monterey engaged in passenger and cargo service from San Francisco to New Zealand and Australia.   —*Matson Line*

SS F. E. WEYERHAEUSER. This vessel named for a member of the famous lumber family was formerly engaged in the intercoastal lumber trade.
                                                    —*Weyerhaeuser Steamship Co.*

SS YAMAHIME MARU. Modern cargo vessel of the Yamashita-Shinnihon Line.
                                                    —*J. A. Casoly*

MV DALERDYK. Running view of the *Dalerdyk* as she steams abreast of Treasure Island in San Francisco Bay.
—*Holland-America Line*

SS WEST IRA. Early freighter of the former McCormick Steamship Company.
—*J. A. Casoly*

SS M. M. DANT. This vessel, named for a member of the Dant family owners of the States Steamship Company, is a C-4 type freighter for the transpacific route from the West Coast. —*States Steamship Company*

SS MARIPOSA. Broadside view of the *Mariposa* in her typical white paint. The *Mariposa* and the *Monterey* have been on the New Zealand-Australian run out of San Francisco and Los Angeles.

—*Matson Navigation Company*

SS OREGON. Modern cargo liner of the San Francisco States Steamship Company fleet.

—*Don Maskell Photography*

MS CANADA. Modern Johnson Line cargo liner in the European trade. Many of the Johnson ships are named for various geographical areas along the Pacific Coast.
—Johnson Line

MS HOOD RIVER VALLEY. Another Johnson Line vessel.
—Johnson Line

SS STEEL APPRENTICE. A fleet member of old-time steamship operation in the world trade.
—*Isthmian Line*

MS TANANA. This vessel is off to the Alaskan fishing grounds with a deck load of gill net boats for Bristol Bay, Alaska.
—*Alaska Steamship Company*

SS LOCH AVON. British cargo vessel in the Pacific Coast-European service. The Royal Mail Line is a pioneer steamship company in the world trade routes.
—*Royal Mail Lines*

SS WAITEMATA. Named for a Polynesian tribe in New Zealand. This ship operated in the Pacific Coast-New Zealand service.
—*Union Steamship Company of New Zealand*

SS ANTONIO PACINOTTI. This fine Italian Line cargo vessel is a representative ship in the trade between Italy, Spain, and Southern France and Pacific Coast ports. —*General Steamship Corporation*

SS TINDALO. A fine, modern cargo liner of the United Philippine Line. The Philippine Government has established a merchant marine since World War II that is growing rapidly. —*General Steamship Corporation*

SS WASHINGTON MAIL. One of the latest cargo liners in the American Mail Steamship Company fleet.
—*American Mail Lines*

SS SANTA FE. Reliable member of the Grace Line cargo fleet engaged in a trade between Pacific Coast ports and Latin America.
—*Grace Line*

SS PRINCESS PATRICIA. Popular sister ship of the Princess Marguerite. The Princess Pat has been in the Alaskan trade service and was formerly in the winter cruise service to Mexico.

—*Canadian Pacific Steamship Company*

SS ORCADES. Another visitor from the British P & O-Orient Line.

—*P & O-Orient Lines*

SS IBERIA. One of the first cruise ships of the P & O-Orient Line to touch our shores. She is presently engaged in another world service out of the United Kingdom.
—P & O-Orient Lines

SS PACIFIC ENVOY. A large British cargo liner in a tropical setting. The Pacific Envoy brings goods to the Pacific Coast from the United Kingdom.   —*Furness, Withy Steamship Co.*

SS ELLEN BAKKE. A Norwegian Company vessel which is presently employed in the Pacific Coast-Far East trade.

—*Knutsen Line*

SS PASADENA. A Scandinavian country ship engaged in Pacific Coast and European trade.

—*East Asiatic Line*

SS LURLINE. Popular Matson Line ship clearing the Golden Gate Bridge while entering San Francisco's harbor.

—Matson Navigation Co.

SS SEATTLE. Johnson Line vessel named for the Pacific Coast city and leading Washington State port.

—*Johnson Line*

SS PRINCESS MARGUERITE. Popular Canadian Pacific vessel presently on the run between Victoria and Seattle. The Marguerite formerly operated the triangle route between Vancouver, Victoria, and Seattle.

—*Leonard Frank*

MS NORTHLAND PRINCE. Modern passenger-cargo vessel in the Northland Navigation service. This ship sails from Vancouver to various ports along the British Columbia Coast.   —*Northland Shipping Co.*

SS FLYING CLOUD. An Isbrandtsen cargo ship which adopted the name of a famous clipper ship of earlier days.

—*J. A. Casoly*

PRESIDENT JACKSON. A round-the-world President Line cargo liner.

—*American President Lines*

TUG LA REINE. One of the recent tugs in the Vancouver Tug Boat fleet.

—*Vancouver Tug Boat Co.*

TUG RESTLESS. Modern sea-going tug towing a fuel barge.
Puget Sound Tug and Barge Co.

SS LOCH LOYAL. A European visitor from the Furness Line of Great Britain.

J. A. Casoly

SS SANTA FLAVIA. A companion vessel to the *Santa Fe* in the Pacific Coast South American trade.

—Mike McGarvey

SS BIEBERSTEIN. A German vessel sailing in the Pacific Coast European trade for North German Lloyd.
—*J. A. Casoly*

SS DIEMERDYK. Another vessel in the European trade to the Pacific Coast.
—*Holland-America Line*

KOCHU MARU. Note the graceful lines of the Daido Line cargo liner.
—*General Steamship Corporation*

SS MORMACLAND. Typical freighter of Moore-McCormack in the Pacific Coast trade.
—*Moore-McCormack Lines, Inc.*

OLYMPIA MARU. Former Mitsubishi Line cargo liner now under the N. Y. K. Line flag.
—*N. Y. K. Line*

MS CANADIAN STAR. View of one of the Blue Star cargo liners which engages in a general and refrigerated cargo service from the Pacific Coast to the United Kingdom and continental ports.   —*Blue Star Line*

KERSTEN MILES. This vessel was in the Pacific Coast European direct service for the Hanseatic-Vaasa Line.
—*Williams, Dimond & Co.*

ARGENTINA MARU. Modern cargo-passenger liner engaged in the transpacific trade for the Mitsui O. S. K. Lines.
—*Mitsui O. S. K. Lines*

MS FRANCE MARU. One of the "K" Line (Kawasaki Kisen Kaisha, Ltd.) fleet vessels which is engaged in the transpacific trade.
—*Kerr Steamship Company*

PRESIDENT HOOVER. *SS President Hoover* when she was sailing under the Dollar Line insignia (1931).
—*Steamship Historical Society of America*

SS EDGAR F. LUCKENBACH. One of the large freighters of the former Luckenbach intercoastal fleet.

—Steamship Historical Society of America

Chapter VII

Steamships and Motorships of Tomorrow.

DOWN THROUGH THE YEARS there has been a decided change in the profile or outward appearance of the steamship. One noticeable change is the number and shape of the vessel's funnel or funnels. The steamship *Great Eastern* had five funnels or smokestacks. Later on, the speedy Atlantic passenger liner the *Mauretania* had three tall funnels. Today the huge express liners have two large funnels and most Diesel vessels have one squatty funnel. The British passenger liner *Canberra* has an unusual arrangement by having two streamlined funnels placed opposite each other at the aft end of the ship. The *Great Eastern,* like the first *SS Savannah,* carried several masts as they had to depend on their sails to finish the voyage. The *Mauretania* of 1907 had two masts without sails, one forward and one aft. The *SS United States* of today carries one mast on the wheelhouse to carry lights, radar, etc.

In building the *Canberra** the engineers added some unusual features to this huge cruise ship. The engines for one thing were placed near the stern instead of near the center as with most ships. It is said this greatly reduces the amount of vibration in the central living quarters of the vessel. Besides the usual gyroscopes and stabilizers to keep the ship from rolling in high seas, the *Canberra* has a unique propulsion system in which the captain can maneuver the ship sidewise for docking. Passenger luggage is handled by means of an electric conveyance and elevators. The *Canberra* is equipped with closed circuit television. There are four swimming pools, including one for the crew. Even the teenagers have been given a special room called the Pop Inn where they have a coffee bar and juke box. The *Canberra* carries more passengers than any other liners when she can accommodate 2,238 first- and tourist-class and the vessel has a crew of 1,000. The *Canberra* and *Oriana* have service speeds of 27½ knots, which is tremendous when one considers they have a gross tonnage of 45,000 and 42,000 respectively.

Many attempts have been made in recent years to design and construct vessels to serve a particular type of trade. Some were built to carry special types of booms and winches, such as the *Philippine Bear* and the *SS President Lincoln,* while the *MS Brimanger* is a smaller and more compact vessel to fit its particular trade.

Many modern cargo vessels have a streamlined effect so popular today in transportation of all kinds. This is represented in the accompanying pictures of the *MS Burrard* and the *MS Rio de Janeiro.*

It is evident that we are living in a push-button age. This is easily seen in our homes, in industry, in the modern automobile, and in many other ways. Ocean-going vessels are now reaching the point of automation in order to reduce the size of the crew and thus the cost of labor.

*The name means "meeting place" in Australia's aboriginal language.

SS CANBERRA. Flag ship of the P & O-Orient Lines of England. The Canberra is presently the largest vessel in the company's fleet and is used in a regular cruising service on a world-wide basis. Note the two funnels side by side at the stern of the ship.

—P & O-Orient Lines

MS RIO DE JANEIRO. Streamlined cargo vessel of one named for a South American port.

—Johnson Line

SS PRESIDENT LINCOLN. "Sea Racer" class modern cargo liner in the transpacific trade.
—*American President Lines*

The *NS Savannah* is a nuclear-powered merchant vessel and is the only one of her type in America. Throughout the world merchant vessels still operate pretty much by steam or Diesel power so the builders adopt other means to automate their ships.

Recently an American vessel by the name of *Mormacargo,* a Moore-McCormack cargo liner, became the latest word in an automated vessel. She is one of the first vessels with a completely automatic remote control system. This allows complete control of the engine room from the captain's bridge. A console operated by dials is situated in the wheelhouse. The engine room has a big control board where the chief engineer and his aides can check all phases of the engine's operation by looking at a series of dials.

The following is an example of a data sheet for cargo vessels of this type as issued by the Moore-McCormack Lines whose vessels also operate on the Pacific Coast.*

"Constellation" Class Cargo Liners
Statistical Data

MORMACARGO

Owner: Moore-McCormack Lines, Incorporated

Builder: Ingalls Shipbuilding Corporation, a Division of Litton Industries, Pascagoula, Mississippi

Cost: In excess of $10,000,000

Size: Length (over-all) 550'9"
Beam (molded) 75'
Deadweight 12,763   Max. draft 31'7"

*See Footnotes for Chapter 7

Light Ship Weight 7,700
Displacement Weight 19,800

Propulsion: Geared Turbines, Single Propeller

Speed: The H.P. and the very fine lines will permit an operating speed in excess of 24 knots.

Passengers: 12

Crew: 35

Design Agent: Sun Shipbuilding & Drydock Co. and Owner

Cargo Decks: 3

Holds: 6

Dry Cargo: 665,300 Bale Cubic

Reefer: Over 40,000 Cu. Ft.

Navigational Aids: Modern Radar
Loran
Depth Sounder
Gyro Compass
Radio Telephone (VHF)

Electronic Controls: Bridge console with electronic control of speed, boiler temperatures, reefer temperatures, and other automatic devices (the FIRST U. S. ship so designed to be launched)

Keel Laid: April 22, 1963

Launched: January 25, 1964

Design Type: C4-S-60a

Newer and larger cargo vessels are being built for Pacific Coast steamship lines. Seattle's American Mail Line's new cargo liner the *Oregon Mail* will be a 12 million dollar ship, some 563 feet in length, and having a speed of 22 knots. She packs a payload having a displacement of 22,625 tons. Like the vessels of tomorrow, the *Oregon Mail* will be automated.

The Fred. Olsen Line, whose cargo vessels are a familiar sight in Pacific Coast ports, has come out with an unusual tanker. It has so many interesting features that it has been called a wonder of the shipping world.

This new 85,000 deadweight tanker carries only 38 officers and men compared to the usual crew of 58 men. The usual navigation bridge is replaced by a five-story glass control tower rising 75 feet above the sea. The navigator's quarters are reached by an elevator. From this tower the navigator can start the engines and steer the vessel as one would a car. The captain has full view of the horizon and he is aided by a television camera in the foremast to cover the blind area directly ahead of the bow. The pool deck features a swimming pool, a nylon netting-covered soccer training deck and other recreational facilities.

Ship experts say that the cargo ship of tomorrow will be larger and faster than those of today. They say a new type of steel will improve the vessel's speed and cargo-carrying capacity. How much speed will be achieved or sought for is an important question. For, operators of ships have often found increasing the speed of a vessel can also increase the cost of its oper-

PHILIPPINE BEAR. Here she is heavily loaded on her way through the Golden Gate to the Orient. Observe the forest of deck cranes that are used in loading and unloading of this vessel. She is operated by the Pacific Far East Line of San Francisco. All the ships of this company's fleet use the word "Bear" at the end of each vessel's name.

—Pacific Far East Line

MS BURRARD. Modern streamlined Norwegian freighter which can handle regular freight, refrigerated cargo and passengers.

—*Fred. Olsen Line*

ation. As ships get larger port facilities will have to be enlarged, and channels and canals will have to be widened and dug deeper.

Whether there will be a revival of the passenger business is another question that often is raised. People of today seem to want to get from one place to another in a hurry. The airplane and the automobile are largely to blame for this. We have already seen where there are fewer passenger liners in the Pacific trade as the years go by. Most American cargo liners of today carry only 12 passengers because of the high cost of personal service that is needed. Passenger travel along the Pacific Coast disappeared in the 1930's. The famous Empress ships of the Canadian Pacific never returned to the transpacific trade after the last World War. Perhaps the present interest by the public in taking a passenger ship one way and flying by plane the other will keep what few passenger ships we have left on the high seas.

For the past fifty years a number of interesting changes have taken place in shipping all over the world. These changes have been noted with regard to a vessel's design, construction, and even the type of trade by which the ship was to serve on the seven seas. We have seen how the first steamships used sails and steam as its source of power as in the case of the first *Savannah*. When larger engines could be installed and larger space given to fuel such as coal, the steamship line acquired a much larger range of travel than before. In other words they could venture farther

away from their home port without having to refuel. The next change began when the coal burning vessels were replaced by oil burning steamships thus greatly extending farther yet the course of travel. The emergence of the Diesel engine as a source of motive power of the ship widened all the more the area for this type of power. And, finally we are on the threshold of a new source of power for a vessel, the atom-powered or nuclear ship of tomorrow.

The American *NS Savannah* became the world's first nuclear-powered merchant ship. Built at the cost of 53 million dollars, this ship is designed to operate without refueling for three years and travel some 300,000 nautical miles. The *NS Savannah* is a 595-foot ship and has a speed of 21 knots. She carries a crew of 110 men and has accommodations for 60 passengers.

Instead of using the ordinary fuels, atomic energy by means of a reactor is used to heat the water in the boilers. The steam drives the turbines which in turn, through various reduction gears, turns a five-bladed propeller at the stern.

For some time now nuclear power has been used in our war craft such as submarines and larger warships. Even the Russians have a nuclear-powered submarine and also an ice-breaker named the *Lenin*. During the early part of 1968 West Germany launched a nuclear merchant ship, the *Otto Hahn*. This vessel was named for a Nobel prize winner who discovered the principle of nuclear fission.

MS BRIMANGER. Compact cargo vessel in the Pacific Coast-South American trade.
—*Westfal-Larsen Line*

SS ORIANA. Another modernistic passenger liner in the same cruise trade as the Canberra. The interior of this ship is panelled in twenty-four different types of hand polished woods from the four corners of the earth.
—*P & O-Orient Lines*

MS PORTLAND. One of several Johnson ships named for Pacific Coast ports. The Portland is engaged in the Pacific Coast trade with Europe.
—*Johnson Line*

Several steamship companies, both American and foreign, have ordered new vessels for their respective trade routes. Some are on the ways at the shipyard, while others are still on the drawing board. Speed and greater cargo carrying capacity will unquestionably be the order of the day. Foreign shipbuilding still outdistances that of ships built in American shipyards.

The ship of tomorrow will see many changes. The container type ship will be the standard cargo vessel of the day. The tanker will be longer and wider of beam. In March of 1968, there was launched in Japan the world's largest ship afloat. This was a 276,000 deadweight ton capacity tanker by Mitsubishi Heavy Industries of Japan.

The passenger liner will assume more the role of a cruise ship during the off season travel. Appeals will be constantly made to lure the traveler into taking a more leisurely sea voyage instead of hurrying through the air. Which type of passenger travel will prevail is anybody's guess, but it looks as though the air liner will be the winner.

PRESIDENT ROOSEVELT. The Roosevelt was completely rebuilt from a former cruise ship the SS Leilani. The Roosevelt is presently engaged in the around-the-world passenger service. —*American President Line*

AUTOMATION FROM THE
BRIDGE. Automatic controls on
the "Constellation" class Moore-
McCormack vessels of today.
—*Moore-McCormack Lines*

SS CALIFORNIA. One of the latest cargo vessels in the States Steamship Company fleet out of San Francisco. This company's vessels sail chiefly in the transpacific trade. —*States Steamship Company*

ENGINE ROOM CONSOLE. An automated console arrangement in the new "Constellation" class of ships of the Moore-McCormack Lines.
—Moore-McCormack Lines

ESSO DEN HAAG. Deck view of a modern Dutch operated tanker in the Saudi Arabia-European trade.
—Arabian American Oil Company

MS NORTH WIND. Coast Guard vessel North Wind in the center of an ice-floe in the Arctic. The North Wind operates out of Seattle replacing the old services performed by the cutter Bear.

—*Official U. S. Coast Guard Photograph*

AUTOMATION ON A MODERN TANKER. An officer takes a sighting in addition to using his modern equipment.
—*Arabian American Oil Co.*

USING THE SHIP'S TELEPHONE AND RADAR. Third officer talks to nearby ship while fourth officer watches it on radar.
—*Arabian American Oil Co.*

SS PRESIDENT VAN BUREN (1). Head-on view of the *President Van Buren* showing the stylized eagle wrapped around the bow. The *Van Buren* is one of the Seamaster class of cargo liners for the American President Lines. She is the largest and fastest American general cargo ship to enter Pacific service.

—American President Lines

SS PRESIDENT VAN BUREN (2). Another view of the *Van Buren* showing the squared-off transom stern. Smoke pipes have replaced the stack on this new, automated vessel. The *Van Buren* has space for the stowage of 30 automobiles. She has a cruising radius of 11,600 miles.

—*American President Lines*

SPEED FLAG FOR TRANSPACIFIC RECORD. *President Van Buren,* world's fastest non-military freighter, broke the transpacific record from Yokohama to San Francisco in 7 days, 15 hours and 6 minutes, averaging 25.55 knots on the 4,678 mile voyage. There were times during the voyage that the *Van Buren* steamed at better than 28 knots.

Because of this accomplishment, the *Van Buren* has the right to lash the proverbial broom to her mast to indicate a clean sweep in the Pacific.

Prior to World War II, it was the Canadian Pacific's Empress ships that broke one transpacific speed record after another. The route at that time was from Yokohama to Victoria.

—*American President Lines*

MS HOYANGER, 9477 gross ton cargo-passenger liner *MS Hoyanger* in the company fleet which operates in the Pacific Coast-European trade, for the Interocean Line.   *Westfal-Larsen & Co. A/S*

PACIFIC FAR EAST LINE CONTAINER SHIP. An artist drawing of one of the new type of automated container vessels being built for the Pacific Far East Line of San Francisco. Known as a Lash ship, she can be completely independent of wharves.

LASH is the designation for "Lighter Aboard Ship," a revolutionary system for carrying cargo aboard ships in lighters (floating containers). LASH dramatically increases the speed of handling cargoes, and cuts voyage turn-around time in half. The entire LASH vessel can be loaded to capacity in 24 hours, compared to 10 days for conventional ships.*

Lighters (floating containers) will be carried to the stern of the ship by the 500-ton capacity traveling crane and discharged into the water. Similarly, and concurrently, standard containers can be handled into barges by the 35-ton capacity gantry crane. Tug boats will move the lighters and containers to discharge piers.*

*LASH, Pacific Far East Line, Inc., San Francisco, California.

—Pacific Far East Line

NS SAVANNAH. First American cargo vessel to operate from nuclear energy which heats the steam to drive the turbines. The Savannah has appeared on the Pacific Coast during a tour of inspection. Today she operates as a regular cargo vessel out of New York in the Mediterranean service.   —*American Export-Isbrandtsen Lines*

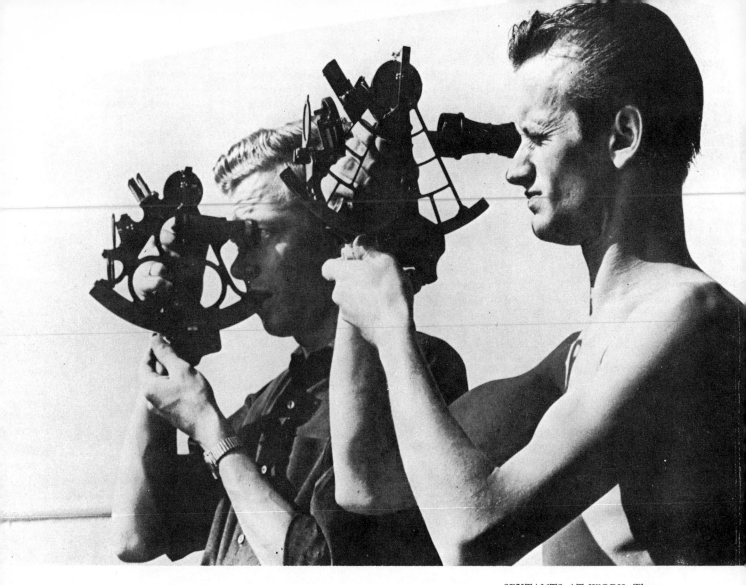

SEXTANTS AT WORK. These men are using their sextants to obtain their ship's position. Very likely they will compare notes afterwards.

—Arabian American Oil Co.

DIRECTIONAL LIGHTS FOR A SHIP? An experiment to expedite navigation by using directional lights attached to the fore mast.

—Holland-America Line

An operator at the San Francisco's Marine Exchange is recording data, or information received from a ship either outside the Golden Gate, or in some waterway in the San Francisco Bay area. The station is located on San Francisco's Pier 45 and has three VHF radio receivers and a high-definition radar scanner among its round-the-clock equipment.

Courtesy of Peninsula Living and the San Francisco Marine Exchange.

IN RETROSPECT

One hundred and thirty years or so of shipping along the Pacific Coast of North America saw many changes. It saw simple beginnings in respect to the appearance of the little *Beaver* down to the fast modern cargo liner of today. There was also a transition during this period, with respect to motive power from combined sail and steam to full steam, thence to diesel and finally to the present-day experiment with nuclear power.

Tremendous changes took place with respect to the size and appearance of Pacific Coast vessels. The original small wooden vessels gave way to steel. There were changes in the length and height of the vessels

down to a development today where large tankers offer a problem as to both moorage and navigation in narrow canals, bays or inlets.

The incentives that helped to develop shipping along the coast were the result of many economic needs. The early incentive for water transportation included such things as fur trading and the discovery of gold. As the land began to be developed, agricultural products in the form of grain, rice, and fruits assumed an increasing share in the export cargo. Then came the lucrative lumber and oil industry, which even today commands a very large share in Pacific Coast shipping. One must not forget the rise of the fishing industry along the coast and Alaska and which has reached tremendous proportions.

Trade routes along America's Pacific Coast followed an interesting development. First, there was the coastal trade from Panama to California and Oregon. Later the coastal route extended from San Diego, in California, to certain ports in Oregon, Washington, and Alaska. Coastal trade in British Columbia included a brisk operation to the many ports in British Columbia waters, in addition to calls to Alaska, to the north, and Seattle, Washington to the south.

At one time, coast trade between the United States and Alaska became more of a steamship operation from Puget Sound ports, with the Port of Seattle serving as a gateway to the North.

Steamboating on the major rivers of the Pacific Coast showed a transition from the combination passenger and freight vessel to a barge operation that is so common today. Highway trucking and the railroad had a large part in the disappearance of the riverboat, not only in the West but in other river systems of this country. Thus the former glamour and color of steamboating on rivers and lakes has just about disappeared from the American scene.

In the very brief account in this book of steamboating on inland waters of the Pacific Coast, two major developments took place. The San Francisco Bay ferries disappeared upon the completion of a series of bridges in the Bay Region of Northern California. While ferry operation on the Puget Sound, British Columbia, and Alaskan waters has shown a tremendous increase in ferryboat service.

The next steamship trade route from Pacific Coast ports headed westward with the sailing of the SS

A new method adopted recently by the San Francisco Marine Exchange for plotting the position of vessels as they move about the Bay Area. It is sort of a console arrangement which registers each segment of a waterway system. For example, the position of ships on the distant Sacramento and San Joaquin river systems may be plotted on the console. Each vessel is identified with a plaque bearing the ship's name and said identification is placed in a slot corresponding to the position of the vessel.

Courtesy of Peninsula Living and the San Francisco Marine Exchange.

Colorado to the Orient from San Francisco, the *SS Miike Maru* from Seattle, and "Empress" steamships from British Columbia. Also in the Pacific there followed an elongated trade route from Pacific Coast and British Columbia ports southward to Australia and New Zealand. The Pacific Mail and Union Steamship Company of New Zealand had a large part in developing this route to the land down under in the early days. In the present century, the Matson Navigation Company began to offer a combined cargo and passenger business to the South Pacific.

The acquisition of Hawaii, first as a territory and later as a state, saw an increasing cargo and tourist trade develop between this "enchanted island" to the United States, which trade has lasted up to this day.

The opening of the Panama Canal in 1914 saw the beginning of an expanding American intercoastal trade between the Pacific Coast and ports along the Gulf and the eastern seaboard of the United States. Both passenger and freight services were developed by various American lines to take advantage of a shorter route between these three coastlines of the United States. This intercoastal trade began to lessen by the middle of the present century. The chief reasons given were competition with American transcontinental railroads and increased Panama Canal tolls. Today there is a limited intercoastal trade which has been enhanced, in part, by the appearance of the container ship.

The Panama Canal also gave considerable impetus to the increase in the Pacific Coast-European trade. Ships bearing the flags from Northern and Southern Europe began to send vessels of their respective countries to Pacific Coast ports. Today this has accounted for a brisk trade between these two parts of the globe. Likewise, a steamship trade has occurred between Latin America and even Africa, and Pacific Coast ports by both American and foreign ships.

Although several foreign steamship companies, generally under European flags, have called at Pacific Coast ports, particularly since World War I, it was Captain Dollar of San Francisco who inaugurated an American round-the-world service from that port. Today the American President Line has a fleet of vessels in this far-flung route. This service includes both passenger and cargo liners. Many American and foreign steamship companies also operate on a schedule that sends their vessels half way around the world from Pacific Coast ports, to the Orient and India and return.

With the new routes and increased trade on the Pacific Coast to various ports of the world, it was noted in Chapter VII that the foreign vessels calling at Pacific Coast ports had outnumbered the American fleet in this same sector of the United States. It is a well-known fact that the American Merchant Marine has lagged considerably behind many other countries, namely; Japan, Russia, and the Scandinavian countries. Many American vessels are now from 23 to 25 years old. In 1964 Japan, for example, had 44 per cent of the world's shipbuilding business. The American Merchant Marine has not kept pace with other foreign nations in terms of replacement. As of 1968, the United States merchant fleet is represented as being only a "sixth-rate maritime power" among the merchant fleets of the world. The high cost of shipbuilding and vessel operation in this country has long been apparent. Failure to provide an adequate subsidy program has long been the chief factor in America's Merchant Marine failure. However, subsidies are not in themselves enough, and are looked upon by some only as a crutch in furthering a merchant marine. It has been suggested that the United States build 50 to 100 atomic power plants for ships and lease them to ship owners. Such an investment would give our merchant fleet the use of fuel that would provide, for one thing, a longer range for our vessels.

The period since World War II, in particular, has witnessed the appearance of highly specialized cargo vessels designed to meet these special needs such as containers, trailers, refrigerated cargo, logs, automobiles, etc. Other vessels have been built to serve particular trade routes where economical operation is important. In the passenger field, specialization also was to be found with vessels being built to serve a particular trade route. In the period following World War I, the auto ferry flourished for approximately three decades on San Francisco Bay, whereas a ferry operation became a continuous and expanding service in the more northern waters of the Pacific Coast. The newer Puget Sound and British Columbia ferries, in very recent times, increased their automobile carrying capacity and also were faster vessels. The Alaska State Ferry System was a success from the very start. Attempts are being made, at this writing, to have one of the ferries operate out of Seattle to Prince Rupert, thus saving a relatively extensive trip northward by car to board the Alaska ferries at Prince Rupert.

Passenger business, in particular, has undergone tremendous change by American vessels on the Pacific Coast. The former passenger trade along this coast and in the intercoastal service is just about nonexistent. The one exception is the booming summer tourist business on the Alaska and British Columbia ferry operation. There is a limited passenger business by American vessels between Pacific Coast ports and Latin America. Here, as is the case in the intercoastal passenger business, the air lines have cut heavily into this former passenger operation.

In the transpacific and South Pacific a limited passenger service by American vessels is again affected by air lines, both American and foreign, traveling in those directions. American passenger trade to Hawaii is experiencing tremendous competition from air travel. The situation for the passenger liner is not entirely hopeless for there will be a day when the traveler will prefer to take a more leisurely trip by water than to fly off into space. The cruise ship of today has greatly instilled the desire for a sea voyage in the face of other inducements to go from one place to another in the shortest possible time.

The 130 years of water transportation along the Pacific Coast of North America have been eventful years and it is hoped that the pleasure and charm of traveling by water will never be relegated to a lowly place in the field of transportation either in this country or abroad.

Footnotes...

CHAPTER 1

[1]METCALFE, JAMES VERNON: "Principles of Ocean Transportation," p. 9, Simmons-Boardman Publishing Corporation, New York, 1959.
[2]Ibid., p. 19.
[3]Ibid., p. 20.

CHAPTER 2

[1]BENEDICT, WALLACE: "The Pacific Mail," *Forum*, November, 1916, p. 577.
[2]LAMB, W. KAYE: "The Pioneering Days of the Trans-Pacific Services, 1887-1891," *British Columbia Historical Quarterly*, July, 1937, p. 145.
[3]BRAYNARD, FRANK C.: "Lives of the Liners," Cornell Maritime Press, N. Y., 1947, p. 174-75.
[4]BAKER, W. A. and TRYCKARE, TRE: "The Engine Powered Vessel," p. 116, produced by Tre Tryckare, Sweden, and published in USA by Grosset & Dunlap, New York, 1965.
[5]"Dollar Line History," Company Duplicated Supplement, 1935, p. 1.
[6]POOLE, ERNEST: "Captain Dollar," *Saturday Evening Post*, May 25, 1929.
[7]Ibid.
[8]MATSONEWS (Commemoration Edition), December, 1943, Vol. 5, No. 4, p. 5.
[9]Ibid., p. 11.

CHAPTER 3

[1]HARLAN, GEORGE and FISHER, JR., CLEMENT: "Of Walking Beams and Paddle Wheels," p. 18, Bay Books, Ltd., San Francisco, 1951.
[2]Ibid., p. 67.
[3]WASHINGTON STATE FERRIES (Mimeographed Brochure), p. 7.

CHAPTER 4

[1]HACKING, NORMAN: "Steamboats on the Fraser in the 'Sixties,'" *British Columbia Historical Quarterly*, January, 1946, p. 1.
[2]"SS *Philippine Mail* is Named Gallant Ship," *Marine Digest*, February 29, 1964, pp. 12-14.
[3]CALKINS, R. H.: "Floundering of the Princess Sophia," *Marine Digest*, August 4, 1951, pp. 2, 22, 23.
[4]"Six Score Souls Go Down to Death at the Golden Gate," *San Francisco Chronicle*, February 23, 1901, p. 1.
[*]BONAVIN, GEORGE: "Shipwrecks Along the Coast of British Columbia" (A Scrapbook of Articles from the *Victoria Daily Colonist*, June 1936 to April 1939).
[5]"Refloating the *Kenkoku Maru*," *The Log*, September 1951, p. 52.
[6]"Capsizes at Seattle Dock," *Portland Oregonian*, March 24, 1933, p. 12.

CHAPTER 5

[1]NEWELL, GORDON & WILLIAMSON, JOS.: "Pacific Steamboats," pp. 70, 75, Superior Publishing Co., Seattle, Washington.
[2]HAYMAN, S. G.: "The Alaska Steamship Story," *Alaskan Sportsman*, p. 60, December, 1960.
[3]HOYE, PAUL F.: "'Tankers: A Special Issue," *Aramco World*, July & August, 1966, p. 3.

CHAPTER 7

[*]"Constellation" Class Cargo Liners, Moore-McCormack Lines, New York.

Selected Reading...

THE FOLLOWING BOOKS are listed here as interesting reading for those who would like more detailed information or background material about ships and shipping along the Pacific Coast.

"Of Walking Beams and Paddle Wheels" by George H. Harlan and Clement Fisher. This is an excellent account of early-day ferries on San Francisco Bay. It is replete with ferryboat history and ferry operation.

"San Francisco Bay Ferryboats" by George H. Harlan. A beautifully illustrated book on the history and development of San Francisco's colorful ferries.

"Paddle Wheel Days in California" by J. MacMullen. A delightful story of paddle wheels on San Francisco Bay and on the Sacramento River.

"Gold Rush Steamers" by Ernest Wiltsee. A beautifully printed book by San Francisco's Grabhorn Press in which the more colorful gold rush steamers of the Pacific Mail and other lines are described.

"San Francisco Bay—A Pictorial Maritime History" by John Haskel Kemble. An excellent story of early-day shipping in pictures and words.

"Ships of the Redwood Coast," J. MacMullen. A delightful book of early-day steamers in the Bay Area and about schooners in the redwood lumber trade.

"Pacific Graveyard" by James Gibbs. This extremely interesting story of shipwrecks is now in its fourth printing. Gibbs' salty description of shipwrecks and the coastal area gives the book a high flavor of the sea and its dangers.

"Pacific Steamboats" by Gordon Newell and Joe Williamson. A most interesting picture book of early-day steamers, particularly those on Puget Sound and in British Columbia waters.

"Pacific Coastal Liners" by Gordon Newell and Joe Williamson. This book extends Newell's original plan to include larger coastal steamer operations. Like the other book, it is primarily a picture book.

Lewis and Dryden's "Marine History of the Pacific Northwest," E. W. Wright. Considered by many to be the "Bible" of ships and shipping on the Pacific Coast. Now available in a reprinted edition.

The H. W. McCurdy "Marine History of the Pacific Northwest, 1895-1965," by Gordon Newell. McCurdy and Newell have carried the marine history from the Lewis and Dryden cutoff date of 1895 down to 1965. Such a work has been long overdue.

"The Engine Powered Vessel" by William Avery Baker and Tre Tryckare. Produced by Tre Tryckare, Sweden, and published in the USA by Grosset & Dunlap, New York, 1965. Perhaps one of the most beautifully printed marine histories ever published. Gives the story in pictures and words from the first powered vessel down to the nuclear ship of today.

"Flags, Funnels, and Hull Colours" by Colin Stewart and published by Adlard Coles of London. Here is a most colorful book in which not only do the ship's funnels and the insignia appear in color but the accompanying house or company flags are also in color. A quick and easy reference book for steamship buffs.

INDEX OF SHIPS

INDEX OF SHIPS

GENERAL INDEX

GENERAL INDEX